SSH: Security and Remote Access

James Relington

DEDICATION

To those who seek knowledge, inspiration, and new perspectives—
may this book be a companion on your journey, a spark for curiosity,
and a reminder that every page turned is a step toward discovery.

AKNOWLEDGEMENTS

I would like to express my deepest gratitude to everyone who contributed to the creation of this book. To my colleagues and mentors, your insights and expertise have been invaluable. A special thank you to my family and friends for their unwavering support and encouragement throughout this journey.

The Origins of SSH

The story of SSH, or Secure Shell, begins in the mid-1990s, during a time when the internet was rapidly expanding but security was still an afterthought in many networked systems. Before SSH existed, administrators commonly used protocols such as Telnet, rlogin, and FTP to remotely access servers and transfer files. These protocols transmitted data, including usernames and passwords, in plaintext across the network, making them highly vulnerable to eavesdropping and man-in-the-middle attacks. In this era, as networks became more interconnected and accessible from virtually anywhere, the lack of encryption presented a serious threat to organizations and individuals alike.

It was in 1995, amid growing concerns about internet security, that Tatu Ylönen, a researcher at the Helsinki University of Technology in Finland, recognized the pressing need for a secure alternative to these legacy protocols. A security breach at his university, where attackers intercepted unencrypted credentials, motivated him to take action. Ylönen designed SSH as a replacement for these insecure methods of remote access and file transfer, focusing on encryption and authentication as the cornerstones of the new protocol. His goal was to create a system that would protect sensitive data from interception, while still providing the flexibility and functionality required by system administrators.

The initial version of SSH, now known as SSH-1, was released by Ylönen as free software, quickly gaining popularity among UNIX and Linux communities. Unlike Telnet or rlogin, SSH encrypted all traffic between client and server using symmetric and asymmetric cryptography, rendering captured packets useless to attackers. It provided an integrated solution for secure remote login, command execution, and file transfer, streamlining previously fragmented workflows. Additionally, SSH supported public key authentication, allowing users to securely authenticate without the constant need to type in passwords. The adoption of SSH spread rapidly through academic institutions, research organizations, and eventually the commercial sector, where its security and ease of use were seen as significant advantages over older protocols.

By the late 1990s, SSH had already become a de facto standard for secure remote administration. However, as usage increased, security researchers identified vulnerabilities in the SSH-1 protocol, leading to the development of SSH-2. Introduced in 2006 by the Internet Engineering Task Force (IETF) as a formal standard under RFC 4251 and related documents, SSH-2 addressed the cryptographic weaknesses of SSH-1 and introduced several architectural improvements. These included more robust algorithms for key exchange, encryption, and message authentication, as well as a modular design that allowed for greater flexibility and future enhancements. SSH-2 also supported features such as connection multiplexing and more advanced public key types, making it better suited for enterprise and large-scale deployments.

The transition from SSH-1 to SSH-2 marked a turning point in the protocol's history, solidifying its reputation as a cornerstone of modern network security. OpenSSH, a widely used open-source implementation of SSH, played a significant role in this shift. Developed by the OpenBSD project in 1999, OpenSSH not only provided a free and secure implementation of the SSH-2 protocol but also integrated additional security features and tools that enhanced the user experience. OpenSSH became the preferred choice for many Linux and UNIX distributions and remains an essential tool for system administrators, developers, and cybersecurity professionals worldwide.

The development of SSH did not occur in a vacuum. It coincided with a broader movement toward securing internet communications, which included the adoption of protocols like SSL/TLS for securing web traffic and PGP for email encryption. SSH stood out because of its versatility and its focus on interactive sessions and automation capabilities. As industries digitized their operations, remote server management became an everyday requirement, and SSH emerged as the most trusted and widely accepted solution for this purpose. Whether used for routine maintenance, deploying software, or managing large-scale distributed systems, SSH provided a level of confidence that legacy protocols simply could not match.

Tatu Ylönen went on to establish SSH Communications Security, a company dedicated to developing and supporting commercial SSH solutions, which further expanded the protocol's reach into enterprise environments. Today, SSH is not merely a tool for remote administration; it is a foundational component of secure infrastructure across sectors such as finance, healthcare, government, and technology. From managing critical cloud services to controlling embedded devices in industrial settings, SSH enables secure access to an increasingly connected world.

Over the decades, SSH has evolved beyond its original purpose, inspiring the creation of complementary tools and workflows. Technologies such as Git, Ansible, and Kubernetes heavily rely on SSH for secure communication and automation. Moreover, as cybersecurity threats have become more sophisticated, SSH has adapted to integrate with modern security frameworks, including multi-factor authentication, hardware security modules, and centralized key management systems. Its flexibility and resilience have allowed it to remain relevant, even as the threat landscape has grown more complex.

The origins of SSH tell a story not only about technical innovation but also about responding to real-world challenges in an ever-changing digital landscape. The creation of SSH marked a critical moment when the security of remote access was elevated from a secondary concern to a fundamental requirement. It laid the groundwork for a more secure internet, one where the confidentiality and integrity of communications could be protected against prying eyes and malicious actors. SSH's enduring relevance is a testament to its robust design, its ability to evolve, and its pivotal role in shaping secure remote access practices that continue to protect networks and users around the globe.

Cryptography Fundamentals for SSH

At the heart of SSH lies cryptography, a field dedicated to securing communication through the use of complex mathematical techniques. Understanding the cryptographic mechanisms behind SSH is essential to appreciating its ability to provide confidentiality, integrity, and authentication in remote access sessions. SSH was designed to overcome the vulnerabilities of earlier protocols, and it does so by employing a combination of encryption algorithms, key exchange mechanisms, and authentication methods that work seamlessly together to protect data as it moves across untrusted networks.

SSH relies on both symmetric and asymmetric encryption. Symmetric encryption uses the same key for both encryption and decryption, making it efficient for securing large amounts of data. However, symmetric encryption on its own suffers from the key distribution problem—how to securely share the key between the client and server without exposing it to potential attackers. This is where asymmetric encryption, also known as public-key cryptography, comes into play. Asymmetric encryption involves a pair of keys: a public key, which can be shared openly, and a private key, which is kept secret. Data encrypted with one key can only be decrypted by the corresponding key in the pair. This dual-key mechanism allows SSH to securely establish an encrypted session without first sharing a secret key in plaintext.

When an SSH connection is initiated, the client and server perform a key exchange to securely agree on a symmetric session key, which will be used to encrypt the bulk of the session's data. This key exchange must be performed in a way that prevents attackers from learning the session key, even if they intercept the exchange itself. The most commonly used key exchange algorithms in SSH include Diffie-Hellman and Elliptic Curve Diffie-Hellman. These algorithms allow two parties to collaboratively generate a shared secret over an insecure channel. Diffie-Hellman, one of the oldest and most trusted methods, uses modular arithmetic and large prime numbers to make it computationally infeasible for eavesdroppers to deduce the shared secret. Elliptic Curve Diffie-Hellman achieves similar goals using the mathematics of elliptic curves, providing the same level of security with smaller key sizes and greater efficiency.

Once the key exchange completes, the client and server derive a symmetric session key, typically used with algorithms like AES, the Advanced Encryption Standard. AES is a widely respected block cipher that encrypts data in fixed-size blocks, providing a balance of speed and security that makes it ideal for SSH sessions. Depending on the configuration, AES may operate in modes such as CBC (Cipher Block Chaining) or CTR (Counter mode), each with its own trade-offs in terms of performance and resistance to specific types of cryptographic attacks. The result is that all subsequent data exchanged between the client and server is encrypted using the agreed-upon session key, ensuring that even if network traffic is intercepted, it cannot be read without access to this key.

Encryption alone is not sufficient for secure communication; data integrity and authenticity are equally important. SSH employs Message Authentication Codes (MACs) to verify that data has not been tampered with in transit. A MAC is a small piece of information derived from the message content and a secret key, appended to each encrypted packet. When the packet arrives at its destination, the recipient recalculates the MAC and compares it to the one sent with the packet. If they match, the packet is considered authentic and unaltered. Algorithms commonly used for this purpose in SSH include HMAC with SHA-2 family hash functions. HMAC-SHA256 and HMAC-SHA512 are particularly common, providing robust protection against common cryptographic attacks, such as message forgery.

Authentication is another pillar of SSH's cryptographic design. Before any commands can be executed on the remote server, the client must prove its identity. SSH supports multiple authentication methods, with the two most common being password authentication and public key authentication. Password authentication, while widely supported, is considered less secure because it relies on the user typing a password, which could be brute-forced or phished. Public key authentication, on the other hand, leverages asymmetric cryptography to provide a stronger, non-interactive method. The user generates a key pair and shares the public key with the server, which stores it in an authorized_keys file. When the user connects, the server issues a challenge that can only be answered by someone in possession of the private key, proving the user's identity without exposing any secrets over the network.

SSH also supports more advanced authentication mechanisms, such as integrating with a Public Key Infrastructure (PKI) or using hardware tokens and smart cards. In these systems, digital certificates and hardware devices further enhance the security of identity verification, adding layers of protection against impersonation and credential theft. Additionally, many organizations implement two-factor authentication alongside SSH's cryptographic methods, combining something the user has (such as a private key) with something the user knows (such as a passphrase) to reduce the risk of unauthorized access.

The design of SSH's cryptographic foundation is also built for forward secrecy, a property ensuring that even if a long-term private key is compromised in the future, past encrypted sessions remain secure because they used ephemeral session keys generated during each key exchange. This is critical in defending against persistent attackers who may collect encrypted traffic in hopes of decrypting it later if keys are stolen or leaked.

SSH's cryptography is highly configurable, allowing administrators to select which ciphers, MAC algorithms, and key exchange methods are permitted. This flexibility is essential, as the security landscape is constantly evolving. Algorithms that are considered secure today may become vulnerable as computational power increases or as new cryptographic attacks are discovered. As such, modern best practices recommend regularly reviewing and updating the cryptographic settings used in SSH configurations, disabling older algorithms such as MD5-based HMACs or legacy ciphers like 3DES in favor of stronger, more resilient options.

In the context of a rapidly advancing digital world, the cryptographic framework within SSH has proven to be a resilient and adaptable shield. By combining symmetric and asymmetric encryption, robust key exchange protocols, and multiple layers of authentication, SSH creates a secure communication channel that has stood the test of time. Whether it is securing remote administration of servers, enabling automated deployment pipelines, or protecting file transfers, the cryptographic underpinnings of SSH remain one of the most important pillars of modern cybersecurity.

How SSH Revolutionized Remote Access

Before SSH emerged as a critical technology in remote system administration, accessing servers and transferring files across networks was an inherently insecure process. System administrators, developers, and IT professionals relied heavily on protocols such as Telnet, rlogin, and FTP to manage remote machines and exchange data. These legacy tools lacked fundamental security features, particularly encryption, and transmitted information like usernames, passwords, and commands in plain text. Anyone with access to the network traffic could easily intercept this sensitive data. In an environment where the internet was expanding and networks were becoming increasingly interconnected, this exposure became a major liability.

The introduction of SSH marked a turning point in how organizations approached remote access. It transformed a landscape dominated by insecure methods into one where confidentiality, data integrity, and secure authentication became standard. SSH's greatest impact came from its ability to seamlessly integrate strong cryptographic protections into a simple and familiar interface. Users could still log in remotely and execute commands on distant systems, but now every piece of information exchanged between the client and server was shielded by encryption. The experience was similar to using Telnet or rlogin but vastly more secure. SSH offered not just protection for login credentials but for the entire session, ensuring that commands, files, and other communications were protected from prying eyes.

This revolutionary shift in remote access security came at a time when threats were escalating. Cyberattacks were becoming more sophisticated, and unauthorized access to remote systems could result in catastrophic data breaches or service disruptions. By implementing encryption from the outset, SSH provided a level of trust in remote sessions that was previously missing. The ability to secure communication over untrusted networks, such as the public internet, without requiring additional software like VPNs or dedicated leased lines, gave SSH a competitive edge and fueled its widespread adoption.

Beyond security, SSH also streamlined workflows by unifying multiple functionalities within a single protocol. SSH was not limited to providing secure shell access; it incorporated tools like SCP (Secure Copy) and SFTP (SSH File Transfer Protocol) for encrypted file transfers. In contrast, legacy tools required separate solutions to handle terminal access and file movement, leading to fragmented and less efficient workflows. By consolidating these capabilities under one umbrella, SSH became an essential utility that improved productivity while maintaining a strong security posture.

Another dimension of SSH's influence is seen in its support for automation and remote management at scale. Prior to SSH, automating system administration tasks across multiple remote servers was cumbersome and often insecure. With SSH, administrators could script and automate critical tasks, such as software updates, backups, and configuration changes, using secure, encrypted channels. The introduction of public key authentication further revolutionized automation. By deploying public keys across servers and protecting private keys locally, administrators could set up passwordless, secure connections for scripts and automation tools, reducing the reliance on interactive logins while maintaining strong security controls.

SSH's role became even more critical as cloud computing emerged and data centers grew larger and more complex. Managing thousands of virtual machines and containers across different geographic locations demanded a secure and scalable remote access solution. SSH proved to be an ideal match for these environments, enabling system administrators and DevOps teams to securely manage distributed infrastructures from anywhere in the world. SSH's portability and support across major operating systems, including UNIX, Linux, macOS, and Windows, further solidified its dominance as the standard for remote access.

The versatility of SSH also extended into the realm of network tunneling and port forwarding. By allowing users to create encrypted tunnels through untrusted networks, SSH enabled secure communication between internal services and external clients. System administrators could bypass firewalls and network restrictions securely by tunneling services such as databases or web applications over SSH. This expanded SSH's role from a mere secure shell into a flexible tool for securing otherwise vulnerable services. Forwarding ports securely through SSH reduced the attack surface exposed to the public internet and made it easier to comply with network segmentation and access control policies.

SSH's open-source implementation, OpenSSH, accelerated its global adoption. Distributed as part of most UNIX-like operating systems by default, OpenSSH provided organizations with a free and well-maintained solution backed by a dedicated security-conscious development community. Its success inspired the broader open-source community and set a precedent for integrating security tools into the default toolchains of modern operating systems. OpenSSH became more than a technical standard; it became a symbol of open, collaborative efforts to enhance cybersecurity.

The cultural shift brought about by SSH extended beyond just technical practices. It raised awareness about the importance of encrypting remote sessions and set new expectations for security in IT operations. Organizations began to deprecate Telnet and similar insecure protocols, with many banning them altogether from production environments. Compliance frameworks and regulatory standards soon followed suit, citing SSH or equivalent secure mechanisms as mandatory for securing remote administrative access. SSH was no longer viewed as an optional enhancement but as an indispensable part of maintaining secure digital infrastructure.

Over time, SSH became integrated into a wide range of modern technologies and workflows. Configuration management tools such as Ansible and SaltStack rely on SSH for securely orchestrating changes across distributed systems. Continuous integration and continuous deployment pipelines frequently leverage SSH to deploy code securely to remote servers. Even version control platforms like Git use SSH to authenticate and encrypt interactions with repositories, ensuring that source code and intellectual property remain protected.

SSH's design choices have stood the test of time, allowing it to remain relevant in a rapidly evolving technological landscape. Its modularity, extensibility, and ability to integrate new cryptographic algorithms have kept it resilient against emerging threats. The advent of technologies like two-factor authentication, hardware security keys, and centralized key management has only expanded SSH's capabilities, providing administrators with more robust tools to control and secure remote access in complex environments.

The revolution sparked by SSH fundamentally altered how remote system management and secure file transfers are performed. By embedding strong encryption, authentication, and integrity checking directly into the communication layer, SSH addressed one of the most pressing challenges of the early internet era. It reshaped remote access from a practice riddled with risk into a secure and reliable component of daily operations, enabling organizations of all sizes to confidently manage critical systems and data across networks.

Key-Based Authentication Explained

Key-based authentication is one of the defining features of SSH and a cornerstone of secure remote access. It provides a robust alternative to traditional password-based authentication by leveraging asymmetric cryptography to establish trust between the client and server. This method not only strengthens security but also streamlines automated processes and enhances user convenience. At its core, key-based authentication eliminates many of the inherent risks associated with passwords, such as brute force attacks, credential reuse, and phishing.

The process begins with the generation of a cryptographic key pair. This pair consists of two mathematically linked keys: a public key and a private key. The public key is meant to be shared freely and is typically copied to the remote server where the user needs to authenticate. It is stored in a file known as authorized_keys within the user's SSH directory on the server. The private key, in contrast, is kept secure and confidential on the client machine. It is never transmitted over the network or shared with anyone. The private key is the linchpin of this system; whoever possesses it can prove their identity to the server that holds the corresponding public key.

When a user attempts to establish an SSH session, the client sends a request to the server, which responds by issuing a cryptographic challenge. This challenge can only be answered by using the private key that matches the public key stored on the server. The client uses the private key to sign the challenge, and the server verifies this signature using the public key in its authorized_keys file. If the verification succeeds, the server grants access to the user. No passwords are transmitted, and the entire process occurs within the encrypted SSH session, further protecting it from network-based attacks.

The benefits of key-based authentication are numerous. One of the most significant is resistance to brute force attacks. Passwords, even strong ones, are susceptible to automated attempts to guess them, especially when users opt for weak or commonly used credentials. In contrast, private keys are usually much longer and more complex than typical passwords, and the cryptographic algorithms that underpin SSH, such as RSA, Ed25519, or ECDSA, make it computationally infeasible to derive the private key from the public key. This resilience dramatically reduces the attack surface for remote authentication.

Another major advantage is the ability to implement passwordless authentication, which enhances both security and convenience. By using key pairs, administrators and developers can log in to remote servers without the need to repeatedly enter passwords. This is particularly valuable in environments where frequent access to multiple systems is required, as it saves time and reduces human error. Additionally, automation becomes far more secure with key-based authentication. Scripts, configuration management tools, and CI/CD pipelines often rely on SSH to perform operations on remote systems. With private keys securely stored and optionally protected by passphrases, automated tasks can proceed without manual intervention while maintaining high security standards.

Key-based authentication also supports fine-grained access control. Since each user can generate their own unique key pair, administrators can precisely manage who has access to which systems and services. If a key is compromised or no longer needed, it can be removed from the authorized_keys file without affecting other users. This decentralized approach to access control simplifies key rotation and revocation compared to managing shared passwords. Furthermore, public keys can be configured with restrictions, such as limiting which commands they can execute or from which IP addresses they can be used, adding another layer of security to sensitive environments.

The format and strength of the keys themselves are critical factors in ensuring secure key-based authentication. Historically, RSA keys were among the first widely adopted for SSH and remain common today, with recommended key lengths of at least 2048 bits to resist modern cryptographic attacks. However, newer algorithms like Ed25519 and ECDSA offer equivalent or superior security with shorter key lengths and improved performance. Ed25519, in particular, has gained popularity due to its speed and resistance to certain types of attacks, making it an attractive choice for modern SSH implementations.

To further secure key-based authentication, private keys can be encrypted with a passphrase. This means that even if the private key file is somehow stolen, an attacker would still need to know the passphrase to use it. Although this introduces an additional step when connecting to a server, SSH agents can be used to cache decrypted keys in memory, allowing users to unlock their keys once per session rather than each time they initiate a connection. This balances security and usability, especially in environments where users frequently access remote systems.

Organizations managing large numbers of systems and users often adopt centralized solutions to manage SSH keys. Tools such as SSH Certificate Authorities (CAs) can issue time-limited certificates that function similarly to public keys but expire automatically after a defined period. This reduces the operational burden of managing static keys and simplifies compliance with access control policies. Alternatively, key management platforms can automate the discovery, rotation, and revocation of keys across the infrastructure, ensuring that stale or unused keys do not become security liabilities.

Despite its strengths, key-based authentication is not entirely immune to risks. Poor key management practices, such as leaving private keys unencrypted or failing to enforce strong passphrase policies, can expose systems to compromise. Keys may also be inadvertently shared between users or reused across multiple systems, increasing the likelihood of lateral movement in the event of a breach. Therefore, it is critical to pair key-based authentication with comprehensive security policies and controls, such as enforcing minimum key lengths, auditing key usage, and regularly reviewing access permissions.

The influence of key-based authentication extends beyond simple remote shell access. Modern workflows, including Git repository interactions and deployment automation, often integrate SSH key authentication to protect valuable assets. Developers use their SSH keys to push code to repositories, while deployment tools use them to transfer artifacts to production servers securely. Even in cloud-native environments, SSH key pairs remain vital for accessing virtual machines, managing containers, and securing administrative interfaces.

Key-based authentication has redefined the security model for remote access by replacing passwords with cryptographically secure keys. Its adoption has become a best practice across industries, from small businesses managing a handful of servers to global enterprises operating large-scale distributed systems. By offering a secure, scalable, and efficient means of authenticating users and systems, key-based authentication has earned its place as a foundational component of SSH and modern IT security at large.

Password Authentication: Risks and Best Practices

Password authentication has long been one of the most common methods for accessing remote systems, including those secured by SSH. Its simplicity and familiarity make it an easy choice for both administrators and users, but this convenience comes at a significant cost. In an era where cyber threats are increasingly sophisticated, relying solely on passwords presents numerous risks. Despite improvements in password policies and enforcement mechanisms, attackers continue to exploit weak, reused, or compromised passwords to gain unauthorized access to critical systems. Understanding these risks and applying best practices is essential for maintaining secure remote access environments.

One of the primary risks associated with password authentication is brute force attacks. In this type of attack, an adversary systematically attempts a large number of password combinations in an attempt to guess the correct one. Automated tools can perform thousands, if not millions, of login attempts per second, especially when targeting SSH servers exposed to the internet. If users select weak or common passwords, such as dictionary words or simple sequences, these tools can quickly crack the password and gain entry. Even moderately complex passwords can be vulnerable if left unchanged for long periods, as computing power and cracking techniques continuously improve.

Another serious threat comes from credential stuffing, a technique where attackers leverage databases of leaked usernames and passwords from unrelated breaches. Since many users tend to reuse passwords across multiple systems and services, attackers often find success by attempting these known credentials against SSH servers. This risk is compounded when organizations lack adequate monitoring and incident response processes, allowing attackers to operate unnoticed for extended periods.

Phishing campaigns also target users with access to SSH-enabled systems. In a phishing attack, users are tricked into revealing their login credentials by interacting with malicious emails or websites that impersonate legitimate services. Even the most secure SSH configuration can be undermined if a user willingly provides their password to an attacker. Social engineering tactics play on human error, bypassing technical safeguards by exploiting trust, urgency, or fear to manipulate users into divulging sensitive information.

Passwords are also inherently vulnerable to interception in poorly configured systems. Although SSH encrypts all data transmitted over the network, reducing the risk of credentials being captured in transit, password-based authentication remains less secure than key-based alternatives. When passwords are transmitted, even within an encrypted session, they represent a single point of failure. If an attacker compromises a server's private key or exploits a vulnerability within the SSH service itself, they could potentially capture user credentials during the authentication process.

To mitigate these risks, organizations must implement strict password policies. Enforcing minimum complexity requirements is a crucial first step. Passwords should be sufficiently long, ideally exceeding twelve characters, and include a combination of uppercase and lowercase letters, numbers, and special symbols. However, complexity alone is not enough. Passwords must also be unique across all systems to prevent a compromise in one environment from leading to a breach in another. Mandating periodic password changes can further reduce the window of opportunity for attackers, though this practice should be balanced against the risk of users resorting to predictable or weaker passwords due to frequent change requirements.

Account lockout mechanisms can be highly effective in defending against brute force and credential stuffing attacks. After a specified number of failed login attempts, the system should temporarily lock the user account or introduce increasing time delays between attempts. This significantly slows automated attacks and raises the cost for adversaries. Pairing lockout policies with intrusion detection systems or log monitoring solutions allows administrators to detect and respond to suspicious login patterns, such as repeated failed attempts from a single IP address.

Limiting the number of users permitted to authenticate with passwords is another important safeguard. Where possible, password-based authentication should be disabled entirely for privileged or administrative accounts. Instead, these users should be required to authenticate using key-based methods or hardware tokens. On public-facing SSH servers, disabling password authentication completely and relying solely on public key authentication can dramatically reduce exposure to common attack vectors.

Multi-factor authentication, or MFA, further strengthens password-based security by introducing an additional verification step. In SSH environments, this often involves pairing the user's password with a time-based one-time password (TOTP) or a hardware-backed security key. Even if an attacker obtains a valid password, they would still need access to the second factor to complete the login process. Implementing MFA across all remote access points significantly reduces the likelihood of unauthorized access and adds an extra layer of protection against phishing and credential reuse.

Server-side hardening plays an equally vital role in securing password authentication. Administrators should configure SSH to use secure cryptographic algorithms and disable legacy or weak protocols. For example, disabling SSH protocol version 1 in favor of SSH-2 ensures the use of modern, secure encryption methods. Additionally, limiting SSH access to specific IP ranges via firewall rules or security groups helps minimize exposure to the public internet and restricts access to trusted networks.

User education is a key component in mitigating password-related risks. Employees and contractors must be regularly trained to recognize phishing attempts and encouraged to follow security best practices, such as using password managers to generate and store complex, unique passwords. A password manager helps users avoid reusing passwords and simplifies the process of managing credentials for multiple systems.

Finally, implementing robust logging and audit trails is crucial for tracking authentication attempts and identifying potential security incidents. Logs should capture successful and failed login attempts, including source IP addresses and timestamps. Centralized log management solutions and Security Information and Event Management (SIEM) platforms can analyze these logs in real-time, alerting security teams to anomalies that may indicate a brute force attempt, credential stuffing, or unauthorized access.

While password authentication remains a widely used and familiar method for remote system access, its security limitations are well-documented. By recognizing the inherent risks and adopting a comprehensive set of best practices, organizations can significantly improve the security of their SSH environments. Combining technical controls with user awareness and process enforcement creates a multi-layered defense that reduces the risk of compromise, even in an increasingly hostile digital landscape.

The SSH Protocol: Under the Hood

The SSH protocol is a sophisticated framework that secures remote access and data transfer by weaving together several cryptographic and networking components. While it may seem simple to end-users who just enter a command and connect to a remote system, under the hood, SSH is a multi-phase process with several layers working in tandem to guarantee confidentiality, integrity, and authenticity. The protocol is designed to be both robust and flexible, capable of securing communications over inherently insecure networks such as the public internet.

When an SSH session begins, the client and server first engage in a handshake process. This is the initial phase, where the two parties negotiate the parameters of the connection. It starts with the client sending a protocol version identifier to the server, which replies with its own version string. This version exchange ensures that both parties are speaking the same language, so to speak, and agree on whether to proceed using SSH-2, the current and most secure version of the protocol.

Following the version exchange, the negotiation phase begins. Both client and server present lists of supported algorithms for key exchange, encryption (also called ciphers), message authentication codes (MACs), and compression methods. These algorithms are then compared, and the most preferred mutual option from each category is selected for the session. This negotiation process allows for flexibility and forward compatibility, enabling different systems to work together securely even if they have slightly different software versions or configurations.

Once the algorithms are chosen, the key exchange process begins. SSH supports multiple key exchange algorithms, such as Diffie-Hellman and Elliptic Curve Diffie-Hellman, which enable the secure establishment of a shared secret over an untrusted channel. During this process, the server also presents its public host key to the client. This host key is critical because it allows the client to verify the identity of the server, preventing man-in-the-middle attacks. The client can compare this host key to one it has cached from a previous session or validate it through another trusted method, such as manual verification or certificate-based trust.

With the shared secret now established, a session key is derived, and symmetric encryption is activated. From this point onward, all data exchanged between the client and server is encrypted using the negotiated cipher. Commonly used ciphers include AES (Advanced Encryption Standard) and ChaCha20, both known for their performance and security. Symmetric encryption is significantly faster than asymmetric encryption, making it well-suited for securing the continuous stream of data during the session.

The encryption layer is complemented by a message authentication layer. Each encrypted packet sent during the session includes a Message Authentication Code, or MAC. The MAC ensures that the data has not been tampered with in transit. The receiving party uses the shared session key to verify the MAC, confirming the authenticity and integrity of the packet. If a packet fails this check, it is immediately discarded, and depending on configuration, the session may be terminated to prevent further tampering attempts.

Once encryption and integrity verification are in place, the SSH protocol proceeds to user authentication. The client must prove its identity to the server before it is granted access. The protocol supports multiple authentication methods, including password authentication, public key authentication, and multi-factor authentication mechanisms. The most common and secure method is public key authentication, where the client signs a server-issued challenge using its private key, and the server verifies this signature using the client's corresponding public key. Other authentication methods can be layered on top to provide additional security.

Once the user is authenticated, SSH establishes a secure tunnel and multiplexes several logical channels over this single encrypted connection. This feature is one of SSH's most powerful aspects, enabling users to run multiple operations within the same session without creating new connections. For example, one channel might be used for a remote shell session, while another is simultaneously used for an SFTP file transfer. Port forwarding, or tunneling, also takes advantage of this multiplexing capability. By forwarding local or remote ports over the encrypted connection, SSH allows secure access to services such as web servers, databases, or other applications running on the remote network.

Compression can also be enabled during the session to improve performance, especially over slow or high-latency links. When activated, data is compressed before encryption, reducing the volume of information transmitted and accelerating the session, although modern networks often make this feature less necessary.

The protocol is designed to be stateless with regard to session continuity, meaning that each new SSH session starts fresh, negotiating cryptographic parameters and establishing a new shared secret. However, within an active session, SSH can re-key or renegotiate encryption parameters periodically. This enhances security by limiting the amount of data encrypted under a single session key, reducing the potential impact of certain cryptographic attacks.

Another important aspect is SSH's extensibility and modularity. The protocol defines clear separation between its major components: the transport layer, which handles encryption and integrity; the user authentication layer, which verifies user identity; and the connection layer, which manages channels and port forwarding. This modular structure makes it easier for the protocol to evolve and adapt to emerging threats and requirements. For instance, newer algorithms like Ed25519 for public key cryptography or ChaCha20-Poly1305 for encryption and integrity have been integrated into SSH as optional components without requiring fundamental changes to the overall protocol design.

SSH also includes measures for session termination and cleanup. When either the client or server decides to end the session, the protocol performs a graceful shutdown, closing channels, flushing buffers, and securely terminating the encryption context. This ensures that no residual data leaks from an incomplete or improperly closed session.

Throughout all these layers, SSH prioritizes security, performance, and versatility. The protocol's ability to combine strong cryptographic protections with practical features like multiplexing and port forwarding has allowed it to become the gold standard for secure remote administration. The intricate handshake, key exchange, encryption, authentication, and session management processes all occur behind the scenes, providing users with a seamless yet highly secure connection. Understanding the inner workings of SSH reveals why it has remained such a trusted tool for protecting remote access, file transfers, and network communications across countless industries and environments.

Configuring Your First SSH Server

Setting up your first SSH server is a foundational step for securing remote access to a system. While the process may seem straightforward, configuring SSH correctly is critical to ensure both functionality and security. SSH servers are typically installed on UNIX-like systems such as Linux or BSD by default, though they can also be set up on other platforms, including Windows. The primary objective when configuring your first SSH server is to enable secure remote login while minimizing potential vulnerabilities that attackers could exploit.

The first step in configuring an SSH server involves installing the OpenSSH server package, which is the most widely used implementation of the SSH protocol. On Linux distributions such as Ubuntu or Debian, this is accomplished with a package manager using a command like apt install openssh-server. On Red Hat-based systems, the equivalent command might use yum or dnf. Once installed, the SSH daemon, often referred to as sshd, runs as a background service listening for incoming connection requests on the default port, which is TCP port 22.

After installation, the next critical task is configuring the sshd configuration file, typically located at /etc/ssh/sshd_config. This file contains the directives that govern the behavior and security policies of the SSH server. One of the first settings administrators should consider is which authentication methods will be allowed. By default, most SSH servers permit both password authentication and public key authentication. To enhance security, many administrators choose to disable password authentication entirely and rely exclusively on key-based authentication, which reduces the attack surface by preventing brute force password attacks.

Within the sshd_config file, settings such as PasswordAuthentication no and PubkeyAuthentication yes are commonly used to enforce key-based authentication. These directives ensure that only users with valid private keys corresponding to public keys stored on the server's authorized_keys files can gain access. Another important configuration is to disable root login by setting PermitRootLogin no. This prevents attackers from attempting to compromise the most privileged account on the system and encourages users to log in as unprivileged accounts before escalating privileges when necessary.

Limiting which users or groups can access the SSH server is another best practice. Using directives such as AllowUsers or AllowGroups, administrators can specify exactly who is permitted to authenticate. This is especially important in multi-user environments where not every system user should have remote access capabilities. Additionally, it is wise to configure the SSH server to listen on a non-standard port, such as TCP 2222 or another high-numbered port. While this does not provide real security, it can reduce the volume of automated attacks that specifically target the default port 22.

Firewall configuration plays a key role in securing your SSH server. Administrators must ensure that the chosen SSH port is open and reachable from the networks and IP addresses that require access while blocking all unauthorized traffic. Tools like iptables, ufw, or firewalld on Linux, or network security groups in cloud environments, allow fine-grained control over which clients can connect to the SSH service. Limiting access to known IP ranges or VPN networks further reduces exposure.

To protect against brute force attacks, it is also advisable to configure fail2ban or a similar intrusion prevention system. Fail2ban monitors log files for repeated failed login attempts and automatically blocks offending IP addresses by adding them to the firewall. This automated response helps mitigate persistent attack attempts and provides valuable protection in situations where disabling password authentication entirely is not feasible.

Key management is another crucial aspect of configuring your first SSH server. Each user who requires access should generate a public-private key pair on their local machine using a tool like ssh-keygen. The public key is then copied to the remote server and placed in the ~/.ssh/authorized_keys file within the user's home directory. The private key remains secure on the local client and should be protected with a strong passphrase. On the server side, it is essential to verify that the .ssh directory and authorized_keys file have proper permissions. Typically, the .ssh directory should have permissions set to 700, and the authorized_keys file should be set to 600 to ensure they are not readable or writable by unauthorized users.

It is important to configure SSH logging to monitor activity on the server. By default, SSH logs are usually written to /var/log/auth.log or /var/log/secure, depending on the Linux distribution. Reviewing these logs regularly helps detect suspicious behavior, such as multiple failed login attempts or unexpected logins from unusual locations. Integrating SSH logs with a centralized logging system or Security Information and Event Management (SIEM) platform allows for better visibility and faster incident response.

Administrators should also configure session timeout settings to reduce the risk of abandoned sessions being hijacked. Settings such as ClientAliveInterval and ClientAliveCountMax in the sshd_config file allow you to automatically disconnect idle users after a period of inactivity. For example, setting ClientAliveInterval to 300 seconds and ClientAliveCountMax to 0 would cause idle sessions to terminate after five minutes, reducing the window of opportunity for unauthorized access to unattended terminals.

In environments where multiple systems need to be administered, setting up SSH agent forwarding may be necessary to allow secure access to other systems without exposing private keys on intermediate machines. However, agent forwarding should be used with caution and only when necessary, as it introduces its own security considerations.

For administrators who require additional security, configuring two-factor authentication (2FA) on top of SSH can be highly effective. Integrating tools such as Google Authenticator or hardware tokens like YubiKeys can add an extra layer of protection, requiring users to provide a one-time password in addition to their key-based authentication.

After completing these steps and verifying the SSH server configuration, restarting the sshd service applies the changes. This can typically be done with a command like systemctl restart sshd or service sshd restart, depending on the system's init system. A quick test from a remote client will confirm whether the server is reachable, whether the correct port is being used, and whether the authentication method functions as expected.

Configuring your first SSH server is not just about enabling remote login but about establishing a secure, hardened access point to a system. By paying close attention to sshd settings, firewall rules, key management, and monitoring, administrators lay the groundwork for a remote access solution that is both efficient and resistant to common attack vectors. Each configuration decision plays a part in defending against the evolving landscape of cybersecurity threats while ensuring that authorized users can safely and reliably manage systems from anywhere in the world.

The SSH Client: Connecting Securely

The SSH client is the critical counterpart to the SSH server, enabling users to establish secure remote connections to systems across networks. Whether you are administering a server, transferring files, or executing automated tasks, the SSH client serves as the gateway through which all secure communication passes. Understanding how to use the SSH client properly, along with its security features and configuration options, is essential for protecting both the client device and the remote systems to which it connects.

At its core, the SSH client is a command-line tool that initiates encrypted sessions with an SSH server. On most UNIX-like operating systems, including Linux and macOS, the SSH client is pre-installed and accessed simply through the terminal by using the ssh command. On Windows, modern versions also include an integrated OpenSSH client, or users may choose third-party tools like PuTTY or graphical front-ends such as MobaXterm. Regardless of the platform, the core functionality remains the same: the client establishes a secure tunnel to the server, authenticates the user, and provides a secure channel for remote operations.

To initiate a connection, the user executes the ssh command followed by the username and the hostname or IP address of the remote server, such as ssh user@192.168.1.10. This basic syntax triggers the client to contact the server on the default TCP port 22. The server responds by presenting its public host key, which is a critical component of the server's identity. The first time a client connects to a particular server, it will prompt the user to verify and accept the server's fingerprint, which is a unique hash representing the host key. Accepting this fingerprint adds the server's public key to a file called known_hosts in the client's local .ssh directory. This mechanism helps protect against man-in-the-middle attacks, as the client will issue a warning if the server's fingerprint changes unexpectedly in future sessions.

Once the connection is initiated, the client and server negotiate cryptographic algorithms for encryption, key exchange, and message authentication, all of which occur transparently in the background. This negotiation process ensures that the session is encrypted end-to-end, protecting the user's credentials, commands, and any output generated by the remote system.

The SSH client supports several authentication methods, with password-based and key-based authentication being the most common. When using password authentication, the user will be prompted to enter their password securely within the terminal. If key-based authentication is configured, the client will automatically present the user's private key to the server, signing a cryptographic challenge to prove their identity. If the private key is protected with a passphrase, the client will prompt for it before proceeding. Many users choose to utilize an SSH agent, a program that caches decrypted private keys in memory, allowing seamless authentication without repeatedly entering the passphrase.

Beyond simple remote login, the SSH client provides a variety of options and flags to customize and secure connections. One of the most useful is the -p option, which allows users to specify a non-standard port if the server is configured to listen on a port other than 22. For example, ssh -p 2222 user@hostname connects to the remote host on port 2222. Using non-default ports is a common practice to reduce exposure to automated scans and attacks.

Another essential capability is port forwarding. The SSH client can create secure tunnels for accessing services running on remote servers or networks. Local port forwarding, invoked with the -L option, forwards a local port to a remote address through the SSH connection. This is often used to access internal web applications or databases securely. For instance, ssh -L 8080:localhost:80 user@hostname will forward traffic from port 8080 on the local machine to port 80 on the remote host, tunneled securely through SSH. Remote port forwarding, using the -R option, performs the reverse, allowing a remote system to forward traffic back to the client.

Dynamic port forwarding, enabled with the -D option, transforms the SSH client into a SOCKS proxy. This allows users to route web traffic and other application data through the SSH tunnel, providing privacy and bypassing network restrictions. For example, ssh -D 1080 user@hostname enables the client to proxy traffic on local port 1080 through the secure SSH session.

The SSH client can also be configured with a user-specific configuration file located at ~/.ssh/config. This file streamlines frequently used connection parameters by allowing users to define host-specific settings. For example, users can specify default usernames, ports, and private key files for particular servers, reducing the need to type long commands. A simple entry in the config file might include Host webserver, HostName 192.168.1.10, User admin, and Port 2222, so that connecting via ssh webserver automatically applies the appropriate settings.

To further enhance security, the SSH client supports strict host key checking, controlled by the StrictHostKeyChecking option. When set to yes, the client refuses to connect to servers whose host keys are not already in the known_hosts file. This forces users to manually verify and approve new host keys, reducing the likelihood of inadvertently trusting a malicious server during an initial connection attempt.

SSH clients also provide support for advanced cryptographic algorithms and settings. Users can specify which key exchange algorithms, ciphers, and MACs to use for individual sessions via the -o option on the command line or within the SSH configuration file. For example, ssh -o KexAlgorithms=diffie-hellman-group-exchange-sha256 user@hostname ensures that only a specified key exchange algorithm is used for that session.

For users operating in environments where additional authentication factors are required, the SSH client integrates with multi-factor authentication workflows. This may include time-based one-time passwords (TOTP) generated by an authenticator app or physical security keys using protocols like FIDO2 or U2F. SSH clients can also interact with hardware security modules (HSMs) or smart cards, providing strong cryptographic protection for private keys that never leave the hardware device.

In enterprise environments, SSH clients are often integrated into automated workflows, such as deployment pipelines, monitoring tools, and configuration management systems. Automation relies heavily on key-based authentication combined with careful scripting to establish secure connections to remote hosts without human intervention. The SSH client's ability to execute remote commands directly using the ssh user@hostname command 'command' syntax makes it invaluable for these tasks. Additionally, the client supports batch processing by disabling host key prompts and enforcing non-interactive modes, which are critical when managing large fleets of servers.

The SSH client is more than a simple tool for remote logins; it is a powerful utility with extensive options that allow users to tailor secure connections to a wide range of scenarios. From administrators managing servers to developers deploying applications, mastering the SSH client's features is essential for ensuring secure, efficient, and reliable remote access. By leveraging its full capabilities and adhering to security best practices, users can confidently interact with remote systems while safeguarding sensitive information from interception and unauthorized access.

SSH and Port Forwarding

SSH is widely recognized for its secure remote login capabilities, but one of its most powerful and often underutilized features is port forwarding. By securely tunneling network traffic through an encrypted SSH connection, port forwarding allows users to access services behind firewalls, protect insecure applications, and bypass network restrictions. This capability has become an indispensable tool for system administrators, developers, and security professionals who need to manage services in distributed and often segmented network environments.

At its core, SSH port forwarding involves redirecting network traffic from one port to another over a secure SSH tunnel. By encrypting the data from the source to the destination, SSH ensures that sensitive information, such as database queries or web application traffic, remains protected from eavesdropping or interception. This makes port forwarding an essential technique when working with services that do not natively support encryption, such as legacy databases or internal web applications.

Port forwarding comes in three primary forms: local port forwarding, remote port forwarding, and dynamic port forwarding. Each serves a distinct purpose and addresses different networking challenges. Local port forwarding, often the most commonly used, allows the SSH client to forward traffic from a local port on the client machine to a destination port on the remote network through the SSH server. This is particularly useful when a service on a remote server is only accessible internally but needs to be reached securely from the outside. For example, a system administrator may need to access a web-based management interface on a remote machine's internal network that is not exposed to the public internet. By establishing a local port forwarding rule, such as ssh -L 8080:internalserver:80 user@sshserver, the administrator can map local port 8080 to port 80 of the internal server, making the service accessible securely through the SSH tunnel.

Remote port forwarding performs the inverse operation. It allows the SSH server to forward traffic from one of its ports back to the client. This is often used when a user or service running behind a firewall or NAT needs to be made accessible from the outside. For instance, if a developer is working from home and needs to expose a development web server running on their local machine to a remote office network, they could set up remote port forwarding. Using a command like ssh -R 9090:localhost:3000 user@remoteserver, the developer can map port 9090 on the remote server to port 3000 on their local machine, making their local web application available to users on the remote network via port 9090.

Dynamic port forwarding extends the flexibility of SSH by effectively turning the SSH client into a SOCKS proxy server. This allows the client to forward traffic dynamically to multiple destinations without setting up individual port forwarding rules. The most common use case for dynamic port forwarding is securely routing web traffic through an SSH tunnel to evade network restrictions or to protect data when browsing from untrusted networks, such as public Wi-Fi hotspots. By running a command such as ssh -D 1080 user@sshserver, the user creates a local SOCKS proxy on port 1080, and their browser or other applications can be configured to route traffic through this proxy. All traffic is then encrypted between the client and the SSH server, effectively masking the true destination from local network observers.

The security benefits of SSH port forwarding are significant. By encapsulating otherwise unprotected traffic within the SSH tunnel, sensitive data that would normally be transmitted in cleartext is safeguarded. This is especially valuable when accessing legacy applications or services that lack native encryption, such as older database servers, remote desktop services, or proprietary protocols.

SSH port forwarding ensures that attackers on the same local network or in transit cannot snoop on this data.

Port forwarding is also a valuable tool for circumventing restrictive firewalls and network segmentation policies. In many corporate or cloud environments, direct access to certain resources is restricted to specific internal networks or VPNs. SSH port forwarding enables authorized users to temporarily bypass these restrictions without altering firewall rules or network configurations. For example, developers who need temporary access to a staging environment database can set up a secure tunnel using SSH, connect to the resource, and close the tunnel once the task is complete.

However, the power of SSH port forwarding comes with security considerations that must be carefully managed. Improper use of port forwarding can introduce risks, such as exposing sensitive internal services to unauthorized users. To mitigate this, administrators should implement strict access control policies and ensure that only trusted users have the ability to create SSH tunnels. Additionally, SSH server configurations can limit or disable port forwarding capabilities altogether for certain accounts or groups by setting AllowTcpForwarding no in the sshd_config file.

Another important consideration is monitoring and auditing SSH sessions that utilize port forwarding. Since port forwarding can be used to tunnel arbitrary traffic, it has the potential to bypass traditional security controls such as firewalls or intrusion detection systems. Organizations should ensure that SSH activity is logged comprehensively and that suspicious forwarding activity is investigated promptly. Some security tools and SIEM platforms can detect unusual patterns, such as unexpected forwarded ports or tunnels to known malicious destinations.

Automating port forwarding through SSH is also common in deployment and orchestration workflows. Configuration management tools and CI/CD pipelines frequently leverage SSH tunnels to securely deploy applications, synchronize databases, or perform remote tasks across network boundaries. Automated port forwarding allows scripts and tools to establish secure communication channels without user intervention, enabling seamless integration between development, testing, and production environments.

Port forwarding can also be combined with other SSH features to further enhance its capabilities. For instance, users can combine port forwarding with agent forwarding to securely access additional servers within the remote network without storing private keys on intermediary hosts. This is particularly useful when working with bastion hosts or jump servers in segmented network architectures.

In modern cloud-native environments, where microservices and containerized applications are the norm, SSH port forwarding continues to serve as a reliable tool for troubleshooting, emergency access, and secure communication. Administrators frequently rely on port forwarding to access Kubernetes control planes, debug remote services, or securely manage cloud-hosted resources from external networks. The simplicity and ubiquity of SSH make it a universally available option, even in complex hybrid or multi-cloud environments.

SSH port forwarding remains a versatile and indispensable tool for securely bridging networks, protecting sensitive data, and enabling remote access to critical services. Its role in simplifying secure connectivity while adhering to strict encryption standards makes it a foundational skill for anyone working in IT, cybersecurity, or software development. As network infrastructures continue to evolve, the ability to confidently and securely tunnel traffic using SSH will remain essential in maintaining flexible, secure, and resilient operations.

Advanced Tunneling with SSH

While basic port forwarding is one of the most recognized features of SSH, advanced tunneling techniques elevate SSH from a simple secure shell into a powerful tool for complex network scenarios. Advanced tunneling with SSH involves creative and efficient ways of routing traffic securely through different network topologies, bridging segmented environments, bypassing restrictions, and even chaining multiple SSH connections to navigate through layered security zones. These techniques are invaluable for system administrators, network engineers, and security professionals who often work with distributed systems, remote offices, and tightly controlled infrastructures.

One of the most commonly used advanced tunneling methods is the SSH jump host, also known as an SSH bastion host. In tightly secured environments, direct access to production systems is often prohibited. Instead, administrators are required to first connect to a secure intermediary server, typically located within a demilitarized zone (DMZ), before reaching internal servers. SSH provides a way to streamline this process using ProxyJump or ProxyCommand options. Instead of manually connecting to the jump host and then initiating a second SSH session to the target server, advanced tunneling allows a user to chain these connections into a single command. For example, with ProxyJump, a user can establish an encrypted tunnel through the bastion and into the target machine with a simple command like ssh -J bastionuser@bastion targetuser@targethost. The SSH client automatically handles both tunnels, preserving encryption and user credentials throughout the path, reducing operational friction while maintaining a secure workflow.

For more complex scenarios, SSH can tunnel traffic through multiple intermediary servers using chained ProxyCommand directives. This is particularly useful when navigating multi-tiered network environments where a user must traverse two or more layers of security zones. By defining a chain of SSH proxies, each hop through the network is encrypted, and no direct exposure to the internet is required for the final destination host. This multi-hop tunneling protects sensitive assets while granting necessary access to privileged users. It also reduces attack surfaces, as each intermediary system can enforce additional logging, access controls, and intrusion detection mechanisms.

Another advanced tunneling feature involves reverse SSH tunnels in dynamic or restrictive environments. Reverse tunnels are especially useful when working with devices behind NAT, firewalls, or networks where inbound connections are blocked. For example, an IoT device or remote workstation may not be reachable directly from the internet, but it can establish an outbound SSH session to a known public server and create a reverse tunnel for remote access. Using a command such as ssh -R 2222:localhost:22 user@publicserver, the device opens port

2222 on the public server and forwards any traffic it receives on that port back to its own local SSH port. A remote administrator can then connect to the public server and access the device through the established reverse tunnel, bypassing NAT and firewall limitations while maintaining encryption.

SSH tunneling can also be combined with VPN-like functionality using tools like sshuttle, which leverages SSH's tunneling capabilities to create a transparent proxy for entire subnets. Unlike traditional VPNs that require complex configuration and specialized software, sshuttle operates with standard SSH and Python, routing IP packets securely through the SSH tunnel. This enables users to access entire remote networks as though they were on the local network, with the added benefit of SSH's encryption and authentication mechanisms.

In addition to forwarding individual ports or creating SOCKS proxies, SSH can also forward Unix domain sockets and even X11 graphical applications. For instance, developers working on GUI-based applications in remote Linux environments can securely tunnel X11 traffic through SSH using the -X or -Y option, allowing them to run graphical programs remotely and have the display forwarded to their local machine. While not as efficient as modern remote desktop protocols, X11 forwarding provides a secure and functional solution for occasional remote GUI access.

A further advanced technique is agent forwarding, where the SSH agent on the local machine is securely forwarded to a remote server over the SSH session. This is useful in environments where users need to hop through intermediate systems to reach a final destination without copying their private keys to untrusted servers. With agent forwarding, the private key remains secure on the local machine, and only authentication requests are forwarded through the tunnel. However, agent forwarding must be used cautiously, as if the intermediate system is compromised, an attacker could potentially use the agent to access other systems. Limiting agent forwarding to trusted environments and setting agent lifetime limits helps reduce the associated risks.

SSH tunneling can also be automated and managed using configuration files and advanced scripts. By leveraging the

~/.ssh/config file, users can predefine complex tunneling setups, specifying jump hosts, dynamic forwarding rules, and custom ports for different environments. Automation allows for consistent, repeatable tunnel setups, reducing errors and improving operational efficiency in critical workflows.

SSH tunnels can even be integrated into hybrid cloud environments. Organizations that span on-premises and cloud infrastructure frequently use SSH tunnels to securely connect resources across different platforms. For example, SSH tunnels can bridge a cloud-hosted Kubernetes control plane to on-premises development machines, or provide secure database access from local tools to cloud-hosted services without exposing sensitive ports to the internet.

Despite the power and flexibility of advanced SSH tunneling, security considerations must remain at the forefront. Improperly configured tunnels can inadvertently expose internal services to external networks, creating unintentional security gaps. To mitigate this, SSH servers can enforce strict restrictions on tunnel usage. Administrators may disable port forwarding entirely for certain users or roles using PermitOpen and AllowTcpForwarding directives in the sshd_config file. For even tighter control, SSH servers can use ForceCommand and restricted shells to limit what users can do once connected.

In modern DevOps and security workflows, advanced SSH tunneling techniques are indispensable. Whether connecting to isolated systems, navigating segmented networks, or protecting sensitive data in transit, SSH's tunneling capabilities deliver secure and reliable solutions. As cloud architectures, microservices, and distributed systems continue to expand, advanced SSH tunnels play an essential role in enabling secure connectivity and maintaining operational agility, while adhering to the highest standards of cybersecurity.

Secure File Transfers with SCP

SCP, which stands for Secure Copy Protocol, is one of the most commonly used tools for transferring files securely over SSH. It provides a simple yet powerful way to copy files between local and remote systems or between two remote systems through an encrypted channel. Built directly on top of the SSH protocol, SCP inherits the same robust security properties, including strong encryption, authentication, and integrity verification, ensuring that files moved across the network are protected from unauthorized access or tampering.

SCP is favored for its simplicity. It operates similarly to the traditional Unix cp command, making it intuitive for users already familiar with basic command-line operations. The standard syntax involves specifying the source file and the destination, such as scp file.txt user@remote:/home/user/, which securely copies file.txt from the local machine to the remote system under the specified path. Likewise, scp user@remote:/var/log/syslog ./ will copy the syslog file from the remote server to the current directory on the local machine. This easy-to-understand interface makes SCP highly accessible, even to users who may not be experts in secure file transfer protocols.

The core advantage of SCP lies in its integration with SSH, which provides confidentiality and integrity for every transfer. Every SCP session initiates an SSH connection between the client and server. This means that the data, as well as authentication credentials such as passwords or private key-based authentication requests, are fully encrypted throughout the process. This differs sharply from older protocols like FTP or rcp, which transmit files and credentials in plaintext, leaving them vulnerable to interception by anyone monitoring the network.

SCP supports recursive file copying, enabling entire directories to be securely transferred in one command. By using the -r option, users can copy directory structures along with their contents, preserving file hierarchy and permissions. For example, scp -r /local/folder user@remote:/home/user/ will transfer the entire folder and its subdirectories to the remote server. This functionality is particularly valuable when administrators need to deploy application files, back up configuration directories, or synchronize datasets between systems.

Performance can also be adjusted when using SCP. The -C flag enables compression during file transfers, reducing the amount of data sent over the network. This is especially useful when transferring large files or working over slow or high-latency connections. Compression helps speed up transfers while still retaining the security benefits of the underlying SSH tunnel. Additionally, users can control the bandwidth usage of SCP sessions by using the -l option, which limits the rate at which data is transferred, measured in kilobits per second. This feature can prevent file transfers from consuming too much network bandwidth and impacting other critical operations.

Another significant advantage of SCP is its ability to perform non-interactive transfers, making it highly useful in automated workflows and scripts. System administrators often include SCP commands in backup scripts, deployment pipelines, and scheduled jobs to securely move files between systems without requiring manual intervention. When combined with SSH key-based authentication, these automated transfers can occur seamlessly and securely, eliminating the need for interactive password entry and reducing the potential for human error.

Despite its strengths, SCP does come with some limitations that should be considered in modern environments. One key limitation is its lack of advanced file management capabilities. Unlike SFTP, which provides functionality for file browsing, renaming, and deletion on the remote server, SCP is focused solely on copying files. It does not offer a built-in way to manipulate remote directories beyond copying files to or from them. This makes SCP well-suited for straightforward file transfer operations but less flexible when full remote file management is needed.

Additionally, SCP does not natively support resuming interrupted file transfers. If a large file transfer is interrupted due to network failure or user action, the process must be restarted from the beginning, potentially wasting time and bandwidth. Workarounds, such as using rsync over SSH, can address this limitation by allowing incremental or resumable transfers, but SCP itself is a simple, stateless tool that performs one-time transfers from source to destination.

Security best practices are vital when using SCP, especially when transferring sensitive files across public or untrusted networks. As with any SSH-based tool, users should ensure that strong key-based authentication is in place, minimizing the risks associated with password-based logins. Administrators should also review and enforce permissions on both the source and destination systems, ensuring that only authorized users can execute SCP commands or access specific directories.

Some organizations may configure SSH servers to restrict SCP usage to specific directories or users. For example, by using restricted shells or chroot environments, administrators can limit where incoming SCP transfers are placed or restrict where files can be copied from. This additional layer of control reduces the likelihood of sensitive files being exposed or overwritten during transfers.

SCP can also be combined with other SSH features, such as port forwarding, to tunnel file transfers through intermediate hosts. For instance, if a server is only accessible through a bastion host, users can first establish an SSH tunnel using dynamic or local forwarding, then execute the SCP command to securely copy files through the pre-established secure tunnel.

Logging and auditing SCP transfers are important in regulated environments where accountability and traceability are required. Since SCP runs over SSH, all transfers are logged as part of the SSH session, typically recorded in system logs such as /var/log/auth.log on Linux systems. Reviewing these logs regularly can help detect unauthorized or suspicious transfer activities, such as unexpected outbound file transfers or connections from unknown IP addresses.

Although newer tools like SFTP and rsync have gained popularity due to their enhanced capabilities, SCP remains a trusted and reliable choice for secure file transfers. It excels in scenarios where simplicity, speed, and compatibility with existing SSH infrastructure are priorities. Because SCP is part of the standard OpenSSH suite, it is almost universally available on Linux, UNIX, and macOS systems, and it is readily supported in automated workflows, cloud-native deployments, and traditional data center environments alike.

SCP continues to hold its place as an essential utility in the toolkit of administrators and developers who need a straightforward, secure method to move files between systems. Whether for ad-hoc file transfers, automated scripts, or deployment tasks, its seamless integration with SSH provides the peace of mind that comes with knowing sensitive data is encrypted and protected during transit, regardless of where or how it travels across modern networked environments.

Using SFTP for Modern File Management

SFTP, or SSH File Transfer Protocol, is a powerful and flexible tool for managing files securely over SSH. While often confused with FTP due to its similar name, SFTP is fundamentally different. Unlike FTP, which transmits data and credentials in plaintext and relies on separate control and data channels, SFTP operates entirely within the encrypted SSH session, providing strong security for file transfers and remote file management tasks. In modern IT environments where secure data handling is a necessity, SFTP offers a comprehensive solution for both interactive file management and automation workflows.

SFTP allows users to perform a wide range of file management operations on remote servers, not limited to merely uploading or downloading files. Through SFTP, users can list remote directories, change file permissions, rename files, create new directories, remove files, and even check file sizes and timestamps. This versatility positions SFTP as a complete remote file system interface, eliminating the need for separate SSH sessions to execute file-related tasks outside of transfers. This capability is particularly important in workflows where administrators and developers frequently manage remote files and need to interact with them in a secure and efficient manner.

The SFTP client is typically accessed via the command-line interface on UNIX-like systems using the sftp command, though numerous graphical clients are also available for users who prefer a visual interface. Popular GUI clients such as FileZilla, WinSCP, and Cyberduck provide user-friendly drag-and-drop functionality while still leveraging the underlying security of the SSH protocol. Whether through the terminal or a graphical interface, SFTP provides seamless access to remote file systems in an encrypted environment, making it suitable for both technical and non-technical users who need to transfer files securely.

A typical SFTP session starts when the user connects to a remote server with a command like sftp user@hostname. The client initiates an SSH connection under the hood, using the same key-based or password-based authentication methods as standard SSH sessions. Once authenticated, users are presented with an interactive shell where they can issue file system commands. Commands such as ls, cd, put, get, rm, mkdir, and chmod are commonly used within the SFTP shell to perform basic and advanced file management tasks. The put command allows users to upload files to the remote server, while get is used to download files back to the local machine. Recursive uploads and downloads are supported using the -r flag with these commands, enabling users to transfer entire directory structures in one step.

SFTP also supports robust file permissions management, which is critical in multi-user environments. By using chmod and chown within an SFTP session, administrators can directly set file permissions and ownership on remote files. This eliminates the need to exit the SFTP session and open a separate SSH shell to execute these commands. For organizations enforcing strict access control policies, this integration is valuable in ensuring that files have the correct security attributes applied at the time of transfer.

One of the defining characteristics of SFTP is its resilience and control over file transfers. Unlike SCP, which lacks the ability to resume interrupted transfers, many SFTP clients and servers support transfer resume functionality. If a large file transfer is disrupted due to network instability or user intervention, users can often resume the transfer from the point of interruption rather than starting over. This saves time and reduces bandwidth usage, particularly in environments where large files such as backups, virtual machine images, or datasets are frequently moved between systems.

SFTP sessions can also be automated for integration into deployment pipelines, backup scripts, and other automated workflows. Using tools such as sftp in batch mode or expect scripts, users can script common SFTP commands and execute them non-interactively. More advanced automation can be achieved by combining SFTP with tools like Ansible or custom Python scripts using libraries such as Paramiko, which allows programmatic access to SFTP servers within secure Python applications.

Bandwidth efficiency is another area where SFTP excels. Compression can be enabled within the SSH session using the -C option, compressing files before transmission and reducing the amount of data sent over the network. This is especially beneficial when working with large text files or across slow or high-latency network links. SFTP also offers better handling of high-latency or unreliable networks compared to older protocols, ensuring a more stable and responsive user experience during transfers and file management operations.

SFTP's flexibility extends to its compatibility with modern security practices. It fully supports key-based authentication, which eliminates the need to transmit passwords over the network. Administrators can enforce policies to disable password authentication and require users to authenticate using SSH key pairs or hardware tokens such as smart cards or security keys. Additionally, SFTP benefits from SSH's strong encryption algorithms, ensuring that sensitive data is protected during transit against eavesdropping or tampering.

In modern cloud and hybrid environments, SFTP plays a crucial role in bridging on-premises systems with cloud-hosted resources. Many cloud providers, such as AWS and Google Cloud, support SFTP for securely transferring files to and from cloud instances or storage services. Administrators often use SFTP to manage application deployments, transfer log files, and facilitate secure backups between cloud and local infrastructure. It is also commonly used in compliance-sensitive industries like finance and healthcare, where strict data protection regulations require encrypted transfers and detailed auditing.

SFTP servers can be configured to enforce additional controls, such as chroot jails, which restrict users to specific directories and prevent them from navigating the broader file system. This is important in multi-tenant environments where multiple users or teams share access to the same server. By isolating each user's session to a confined directory, organizations reduce the risk of accidental or intentional access to files belonging to other users.

Monitoring and logging SFTP sessions is another important security consideration. Because SFTP sessions operate over SSH, they are subject to the same centralized logging and auditing capabilities provided by SSH server logs. Security teams can track who is transferring files, when the transfers occur, and from which IP addresses the sessions originate. This visibility is essential for maintaining accountability and meeting regulatory compliance requirements.

SFTP remains an indispensable tool in the modern IT landscape. Its balance of security, versatility, and ease of use makes it suitable for a wide range of file management tasks, from individual file transfers to complex automation pipelines. Whether used interactively by administrators managing server file systems or as part of automated workflows in cloud-native environments, SFTP provides the foundation for secure and efficient file operations in today's interconnected world.

SSH Agent Forwarding: Benefits and Dangers

SSH agent forwarding is a powerful and convenient feature that allows users to securely use their SSH keys across multiple systems without physically copying the private key to remote servers. This mechanism is widely used by system administrators and developers who need to jump through one or more intermediary servers, also known as bastion hosts or jump boxes, before reaching their final destination systems. At its core, SSH agent forwarding forwards the user's authentication requests through the SSH session to the agent running on the local machine. This means that the private key never leaves the user's workstation, yet it can still be used to authenticate on other machines accessed via the intermediary host.

The primary benefit of SSH agent forwarding is convenience. In environments where users manage multiple remote systems behind a bastion host or firewall, agent forwarding simplifies the workflow. Instead of copying private keys to each intermediary system, which could pose a severe security risk, users forward their authentication agent. This allows them to seamlessly hop from one server to another while still using their original SSH key to authenticate, without storing the key on remote servers. This is particularly useful in highly segmented network architectures where direct access to internal servers is prohibited and users must first connect to a jump host that serves as a controlled access point.

Agent forwarding also improves efficiency, especially in dynamic or large-scale environments. For example, system administrators managing fleets of servers across cloud, on-premises, or hybrid infrastructures often rely on agent forwarding to simplify remote management tasks. Developers working on distributed applications can also benefit when deploying or debugging code on different layers of a network. The ability to authenticate smoothly across multiple hops saves time, reduces complexity, and supports automation when chaining commands or executing scripts across interconnected servers.

Another advantage is that agent forwarding helps maintain key confidentiality. By keeping the private key on the local machine and forwarding only the authentication requests, users reduce the chances of key theft on untrusted or less secure intermediary servers. Since the key never resides on remote hosts, it is less likely to be compromised in case one of the intermediary machines is breached or infected with malware.

Despite these benefits, SSH agent forwarding is not without its risks, and if misused, it can introduce serious security vulnerabilities into a system. The most significant danger arises from trusting the remote servers where the forwarded agent is available. When agent forwarding is enabled, any user or process on the intermediary server with sufficient privileges can access the forwarded SSH agent. In a worst-case scenario, an attacker who gains control of a bastion host or another intermediary server can hijack the forwarded agent and use it to authenticate against other servers where the user's key is trusted.

Unlike physical key theft, where an attacker must first obtain the private key file itself, agent hijacking allows malicious actors to issue authentication requests via the forwarded agent without ever extracting the private key. This means that a compromised bastion host or remote system could be leveraged as a pivot point to escalate access throughout an environment, moving laterally to other systems that trust the user's key.

Another potential issue is the lack of fine-grained control over forwarded agent usage. Once forwarded, the agent typically accepts any authentication request from the intermediary server, regardless of which target server it is destined for. Without additional controls, this could inadvertently allow forwarded authentication to be used for unintended purposes, such as connecting to sensitive servers or services outside the scope of the original workflow.

To mitigate the risks associated with agent forwarding, users and administrators should adopt several best practices. The first is to avoid using agent forwarding on untrusted or public servers. Agent forwarding should only be enabled in secure environments where the integrity of intermediary systems can be assured. In situations where bastion hosts are necessary, these systems should be treated as critical infrastructure components, hardened against attack, closely monitored, and regularly audited.

Another recommended practice is to restrict the lifetime of the forwarded agent session. By configuring the local SSH agent with timeout settings, such as using ssh-add -t, users can ensure that keys cached in the agent expire automatically after a certain period. This reduces the window of opportunity for exploitation if an attacker gains control of an intermediary system while the agent is still forwarded and active.

Additionally, some SSH agents support confirmation prompts, which require the user to manually approve each authentication request before it is processed by the forwarded agent. While this introduces some friction into the workflow, it offers an extra layer of protection by preventing unauthorized or automated use of the forwarded agent. Tools such as gpg-agent or the OpenSSH agent can be configured to prompt users before allowing each signature operation.

Another layer of defense is to leverage advanced SSH configurations, such as restricting agent forwarding to specific hosts in the SSH client configuration file. By setting ForwardAgent to yes only for known, trusted hosts within the ~/.ssh/config file, users can reduce the risk of accidentally forwarding the agent to insecure environments. For example, ForwardAgent yes can be applied only to designated bastion hosts rather than to all outbound SSH connections.

In modern cloud and enterprise environments, many organizations are also moving toward centralized key management and short-lived certificates as alternatives to agent forwarding. Solutions such as SSH Certificate Authorities (CAs) issue temporary credentials that expire automatically after a set period, eliminating the need to forward persistent SSH agents across multiple systems. Some security-conscious environments combine this approach with bastion hosts and privileged access management (PAM) solutions, further reducing the attack surface of remote access workflows.

Agent forwarding, when used responsibly and within secure architectures, remains a valuable tool that simplifies complex SSH workflows and improves operational efficiency. However, understanding the potential dangers is essential to using this feature safely. Striking a balance between convenience and security requires careful planning, adherence to best practices, and an awareness of the environment in which the agent is being forwarded.

By properly securing intermediary systems, limiting agent exposure, and adopting complementary security measures, organizations and users can harness the full potential of SSH agent forwarding without introducing unnecessary risk. It remains a critical tool in modern IT and DevOps practices, enabling secure and streamlined access across distributed systems, provided that its usage is carefully controlled and continuously monitored.

Managing SSH Keys at Scale

As organizations grow and IT environments become more complex, the challenge of managing SSH keys at scale becomes a significant concern for security and operational teams. While using SSH keys is a best practice for secure remote access, the proliferation of thousands or even millions of SSH key pairs across servers, users, and automated systems can introduce serious risks if not managed properly. Without an effective strategy, organizations may face issues such as unauthorized access, key sprawl, orphaned keys, and compliance violations. Managing SSH keys at scale requires a systematic approach that balances security, operational efficiency, and compliance requirements.

The first challenge arises from the sheer volume of keys that accumulate over time. In a typical large enterprise, each administrator, developer, service account, and automated system may have its own key pair. These keys are often distributed across multiple servers, cloud environments, and virtual machines. In dynamic environments, such as those relying on cloud-native architectures or DevOps practices, the rate at which keys are created, used, and discarded can increase exponentially. Without centralized oversight, organizations lose visibility into where keys are deployed, who owns them, and whether they remain in active use.

A key risk in unmanaged environments is the presence of orphaned keys. These are public keys residing on servers that no longer have an active or authorized user associated with them. Orphaned keys often result from employee turnover, role changes, or system decommissioning. If left unattended, these keys can create backdoors for former employees, contractors, or malicious actors to regain access to critical systems. In the absence of regular key audits, orphaned keys often go unnoticed for extended periods, undermining even the most robust perimeter defenses.

Key sprawl also contributes to poor operational hygiene. When administrators or users generate new key pairs for each system or project without a centralized management process, the number of unmanaged keys grows rapidly. This makes it difficult to track key usage, enforce policies such as key expiration or rotation, and ensure compliance with security standards. Over time, the resulting disorganization can delay incident response, complicate troubleshooting, and introduce additional administrative overhead.

One of the most effective ways to address these challenges is to implement centralized SSH key management. Centralized management platforms provide visibility into where keys reside, who owns them, and what systems they provide access to. These platforms often integrate with identity and access management (IAM) solutions, allowing organizations to align SSH key usage with user identities and roles. This helps enforce the principle of least privilege, ensuring that users and systems only have the access required for their specific tasks.

Centralized key management platforms also streamline key lifecycle operations, including generation, distribution, rotation, and revocation. Instead of manually copying public keys to authorized_keys files on each server, administrators can automate this process through policy-based controls. For example, when a new user is onboarded, their public key can be automatically deployed to the appropriate systems based on their role, department, or project. Conversely, when a user leaves the organization or no longer requires access, their key can be immediately removed from all relevant systems, eliminating orphaned keys.

Another important aspect of managing SSH keys at scale is enforcing key policies. Security-conscious organizations require key pairs to meet specific criteria, such as minimum key lengths, approved cryptographic algorithms, and passphrase protection for private keys. By using centralized management tools, administrators can automatically reject weak or non-compliant keys and enforce the use of stronger alternatives like Ed25519 or ECDSA over older, less secure algorithms such as RSA with short key lengths. Centralized policies can also require periodic key rotation to minimize the risk of key exposure over time.

Many organizations operating at scale integrate SSH certificate authorities (CAs) into their key management strategy. SSH certificates provide a scalable alternative to managing static public keys by allowing administrators to issue time-limited certificates that authenticate users or systems. When a certificate expires, it can no longer be used to establish SSH connections, reducing the need for manual key revocation. This approach enhances security by shortening the lifespan of authentication credentials and aligning more closely with modern practices seen in TLS/SSL ecosystems.

Automation plays a critical role in managing SSH keys across large environments. Infrastructure as Code (IaC) tools such as Ansible, Terraform, and Puppet can be leveraged to automate the deployment of authorized keys and the configuration of SSH servers. By codifying key distribution and access policies, organizations ensure consistency across environments and reduce the likelihood of human error. Automation also simplifies compliance with industry standards and regulatory frameworks, which often mandate strict controls around privileged access and credential management.

Visibility and auditing are essential components of any large-scale SSH key management program. Organizations must maintain detailed records of key usage, including when keys are created, who owns them, where they are deployed, and when they are revoked or rotated. Logging tools and SIEM platforms can be configured to monitor SSH activity and correlate it with identity data, providing security teams with actionable insights. Regular audits should be conducted to verify that only approved keys are present on systems and that all access aligns with organizational policies.

Education and awareness are also critical when managing SSH keys at scale. Users must be trained to follow best practices, such as securing private keys with strong passphrases, using key agents responsibly, and avoiding insecure behaviors like copying private keys to remote servers. Security teams should provide guidelines for key generation, usage, and secure storage, particularly in environments where users may need to generate and manage their own keys.

In hybrid and multi-cloud environments, managing SSH keys at scale becomes even more complex. Organizations must contend with a mix of on-premises systems, cloud virtual machines, containers, and ephemeral instances. Each of these assets may have unique key distribution and access requirements. To address this, modern key management solutions often integrate directly with cloud provider IAM services and APIs, enabling automated key injection during instance creation and lifecycle management.

Ultimately, managing SSH keys at scale is about balancing security with operational efficiency. Without proper oversight, the sprawl of unmanaged keys can create systemic vulnerabilities that threaten the integrity of critical systems. By implementing centralized management platforms, enforcing key policies, automating lifecycle processes, and maintaining continuous visibility, organizations can secure their SSH environments while supporting the demands of modern, dynamic infrastructure. In doing so, they reduce risk, enhance compliance, and improve the overall resilience of their IT operations.

SSH and Certificate Authorities

As organizations scale their infrastructure, the limitations of traditional SSH key-based authentication become increasingly evident. Managing a vast number of static public keys across thousands of servers and user accounts can quickly become unmanageable. To address this challenge, SSH certificate authorities (CAs) were introduced as a scalable and secure solution to streamline identity verification and access management across large environments. Instead of deploying individual public keys to every server, organizations can use SSH certificates signed by a trusted CA, simplifying key distribution and enhancing security.

An SSH certificate authority acts as a trusted entity that digitally signs SSH keys to create certificates. These certificates validate that a user or host has been authenticated by the CA and can be trusted by any server configured to recognize the CA's signature. In this model, the trust is shifted from individual static keys to the CA itself. Servers no longer need to maintain sprawling authorized_keys files with hundreds or thousands of user keys. Instead, they are configured to trust the CA's public key, and any user presenting a valid certificate signed by that CA is granted access according to defined policies.

The process of issuing SSH certificates starts with the generation of a traditional key pair by the user. The public key is then submitted to the CA, which verifies the identity of the user and signs the key, embedding metadata into the resulting certificate. This metadata can include user-specific information such as a username, role, or group, as well as access restrictions and expiration dates. Once signed, the certificate is returned to the user, who uses it in place of their regular public key when connecting to servers. During the SSH handshake, the server checks the certificate's signature against the trusted CA key and, if valid, permits access.

One of the key benefits of using SSH certificates is the ability to enforce short-lived authentication credentials. Traditional SSH public keys remain valid indefinitely unless manually revoked or removed from the server, creating potential security risks if the key is lost, compromised, or orphaned. In contrast, SSH certificates can be issued with strict expiration times, often ranging from a few hours to a few days. Once expired, the certificate is no longer valid for authentication, dramatically reducing the attack window even if a certificate is stolen.

Another important advantage is the reduced administrative overhead. By centralizing trust to the CA, system administrators no longer need to manually distribute or revoke user keys on each server. Instead, they only need to maintain the CA's public key on each system, significantly simplifying operations. This is particularly valuable in dynamic environments where servers and virtual machines are constantly being provisioned and decommissioned. Newly created instances can immediately trust certificates signed by the organization's CA without requiring complex key distribution processes.

SSH CAs also enable fine-grained access controls directly within the certificate. Administrators can embed critical options into the certificate's metadata, defining restrictions such as the specific servers a certificate is valid for, the commands the user is allowed to execute, or whether port forwarding and agent forwarding are permitted. For example, a certificate could be issued that limits a user to accessing only a subset of servers within a production environment while allowing broader access in staging or development environments. This level of control enhances compliance with the principle of least privilege and reduces the risk of unauthorized lateral movement within an organization's infrastructure.

In addition to user certificates, SSH certificate authorities can issue host certificates. These are used to authenticate servers to clients during the SSH handshake, mitigating the risks associated with trusting static server host keys. In environments without a CA, users often encounter warnings about unknown or changed host keys, which can lead to security fatigue and the blind acceptance of potentially dangerous keys. By deploying host certificates signed by a trusted CA, users can automatically verify the authenticity of servers, improving security and streamlining the user experience.

Implementing an SSH CA requires careful planning and the right tooling. OpenSSH, one of the most widely used SSH implementations, includes built-in support for creating and managing CAs. The ssh-keygen utility can be used to generate a CA key pair and to sign user or host keys to create certificates. Administrators must then distribute the CA's public key to all trusted servers, typically by placing it in the /etc/ssh/trusted-user-ca-keys.pem or /etc/ssh/trusted-host-ca-keys.pem file and updating the sshd_config file accordingly.

Automation plays a critical role in the effective deployment and operation of SSH CAs. Many organizations integrate CA workflows with their identity management systems or ticketing platforms to automate certificate issuance. For example, when a user requests access to a system, the request can be approved through an access control process, triggering the automated issuance of a short-lived certificate by the CA. This helps align certificate issuance with the organization's security and compliance processes, ensuring that access is only granted to properly authorized users and for predefined periods.

Security practices surrounding SSH certificate authorities are paramount. The CA's private key is a highly sensitive asset and must be protected with the highest level of security controls. It should be stored in a secure hardware security module (HSM) or a dedicated, isolated server with strict access controls and auditing. Compromise of the CA's private key would undermine the entire trust model, as attackers could issue fraudulent certificates. For this reason, some organizations use a two-tier CA hierarchy, with an offline root CA that signs one or more online subordinate CAs responsible for day-to-day operations.

SSH certificates also integrate well with modern security frameworks such as zero trust architectures. In zero trust models, the assumption is that no user or system is inherently trusted, and all access requests must be continuously verified. The ability to issue short-lived SSH certificates fits this approach perfectly, enabling organizations to enforce ephemeral credentials as part of their dynamic access controls. Combined with multi-factor authentication (MFA) and identity-aware proxies, SSH CAs enhance both the security and agility of remote access workflows.

The adoption of SSH certificate authorities continues to grow, especially in sectors where compliance, scalability, and security are critical. Financial institutions, government agencies, and cloud service providers increasingly rely on SSH CAs to manage complex infrastructures with thousands of users and systems. The combination of centralized trust, policy enforcement, and credential expiration offered by SSH CAs makes them a compelling solution for organizations seeking to modernize their SSH access models and reduce the operational burden of managing individual SSH keys.

By leveraging the power of SSH certificate authorities, organizations can significantly improve the security and manageability of their remote access environment. This approach allows for a scalable, flexible, and secure authentication system that supports modern DevOps practices, cloud-native architectures, and regulatory compliance requirements, while reducing the inherent risks associated with unmanaged static key sprawl.

SSH in Cloud Environments

As organizations migrate to the cloud and embrace hybrid or multi-cloud architectures, SSH remains one of the foundational tools for secure remote access and management of cloud-based infrastructure. Whether dealing with virtual machines, containerized workloads, or serverless functions, SSH continues to play a crucial role in maintaining operational control over cloud assets. Its ability to provide encrypted connections, robust authentication mechanisms, and flexible tunneling capabilities makes it indispensable for administrators, developers, and security teams operating in cloud environments.

In cloud computing, virtual machines are frequently deployed across services such as Amazon EC2, Google Compute Engine, Microsoft Azure Virtual Machines, and other Infrastructure-as-a-Service (IaaS) platforms. These instances are often spun up and terminated dynamically, depending on the workload demands. SSH provides the primary means by which administrators connect to these virtual machines for setup, configuration, troubleshooting, and routine maintenance. Unlike traditional data centers where servers are often static, cloud-based systems require a more dynamic approach to managing SSH access due to the transient nature of virtual instances.

Cloud providers simplify the process of provisioning SSH access by integrating key management into instance creation workflows. When launching a new instance, users can typically specify an existing SSH public key or generate a new key pair through the provider's console. The public key is automatically injected into the instance's authorized_keys file, enabling immediate secure access once the instance is live. This seamless integration reduces the need for manual key distribution and accelerates the provisioning of infrastructure.

The elasticity of cloud environments also presents new challenges for managing SSH access at scale. As virtual machines are created and destroyed frequently, organizations must maintain strict controls over who has access to which resources. This has led to the growing adoption of automation tools such as Terraform, Ansible, and CloudFormation to standardize instance deployment and key distribution. These tools integrate with cloud APIs to ensure that SSH keys are programmatically assigned and revoked, reducing the likelihood of human error and improving security posture.

SSH is not limited to virtual machine access in the cloud. It also plays a vital role in enabling secure communication between workloads and services running inside virtual private clouds (VPCs) or across hybrid environments that span on-premises data centers and public clouds. Administrators commonly use SSH tunnels to create encrypted links between internal cloud services and external clients or other remote systems. For example, a developer might set up a local port forwarding rule via SSH to securely access a database hosted on a private subnet in a cloud VPC, bypassing the need to expose the service to the public internet.

In multi-cloud and hybrid architectures, SSH also supports the establishment of secure bridges between different cloud providers or between cloud and on-premises resources. Through bastion hosts or jump boxes, SSH enables secure, auditable access to internal systems without requiring public IP addresses for every virtual machine. Bastion hosts are typically hardened, centrally managed servers located within the cloud environment's DMZ, acting as secure gateways through which all administrative SSH traffic flows. By limiting direct access and funneling connections through a bastion host, organizations can better monitor and control access to sensitive cloud assets.

Cloud-native environments often introduce additional complexities for SSH. Container orchestration platforms like Kubernetes may reduce the need for direct SSH access to individual nodes by encouraging automated deployments and declarative management through APIs. However, SSH remains a critical tool for troubleshooting, node-level maintenance, and managing the underlying infrastructure where Kubernetes clusters run. Cloud-based Kubernetes services, such as Amazon EKS, Google GKE, and Azure AKS, typically allow SSH access to worker nodes, which can be invaluable during incident response or when resolving infrastructure-level issues.

SSH is also integral to many DevOps workflows in cloud environments. Continuous integration and continuous deployment (CI/CD) pipelines often rely on SSH to securely deploy application artifacts to cloud-hosted servers or to execute remote commands as part of build and deployment stages. Automation platforms use SSH to push code changes, synchronize files, and trigger configuration updates across distributed cloud workloads. This secure channel ensures that sensitive operations, such as production deployments, occur over encrypted connections, protecting against data interception and unauthorized access.

With the rise of Infrastructure as Code (IaC) practices, organizations increasingly integrate SSH into automated provisioning scripts. Tools like Ansible and SaltStack use SSH to orchestrate and configure infrastructure across cloud regions and providers. This automation is crucial for managing the scale and complexity of cloud environments, where hundreds or thousands of virtual machines may need to be configured and updated consistently. By using SSH in tandem with IaC, teams can enforce standardized security baselines, deploy applications faster, and reduce operational overhead.

Security is paramount when using SSH in cloud environments. Organizations must carefully manage SSH key distribution, rotation, and revocation to reduce the risk of unauthorized access. Cloud providers offer native integrations with identity and access management (IAM) services to improve control over SSH access. For instance, some providers allow users to authenticate to virtual machines using IAM credentials and temporary SSH certificates instead of long-lived static keys. This reduces the attack surface and simplifies key management by integrating with centralized identity systems.

To further enhance security, organizations often implement additional layers of protection such as multi-factor authentication (MFA) for bastion host access, enforcing least-privilege policies, and using security groups or firewall rules to restrict SSH access to specific IP ranges. Centralized logging of SSH sessions is another critical control, enabling organizations to track user activities, detect anomalies, and respond to potential security incidents. In highly regulated industries, SSH session recording and auditing are frequently required to meet compliance standards.

Cloud-native solutions are also evolving to complement SSH usage. For example, some platforms now offer session managers that enable users to connect to virtual machines securely without requiring direct SSH access or open inbound ports. These session managers often operate through secure web-based consoles or agent-based systems that run within the cloud provider's infrastructure, abstracting SSH access while retaining encryption and authentication mechanisms.

Despite the evolution of cloud-native access tools, SSH continues to play an essential role due to its versatility, portability, and reliability. It remains a vital tool for operations teams to troubleshoot incidents, perform emergency maintenance, and manage custom or legacy applications running on cloud-based virtual machines. Its widespread support across all major cloud providers and operating systems ensures that it will remain a foundational technology in cloud infrastructure management.

SSH has adapted well to the demands of modern cloud environments, providing a secure, flexible, and efficient means to manage cloud-based resources. As organizations continue to expand their presence in the cloud, the ability to effectively manage SSH connections, automate key workflows, and integrate with cloud-native security controls will remain central to maintaining secure and resilient cloud operations.

Automating Tasks with SSH

SSH is not only a tool for interactive remote login but also a foundational technology for automating tasks across distributed systems. Its ability to securely execute commands and transfer files without requiring manual intervention makes it invaluable in modern IT environments where speed, consistency, and efficiency are paramount. By integrating SSH into scripts, pipelines, and configuration management tools, system administrators and DevOps teams can automate a wide range of operational tasks, from server provisioning and configuration to application deployment and system maintenance.

One of the simplest forms of automation with SSH involves embedding SSH commands directly within shell scripts. For example, administrators often use bash scripts containing ssh user@server commands to remotely execute routine maintenance tasks such as restarting services, updating packages, or managing user accounts. These scripts can be scheduled using tools like cron to run at specified intervals, automating repetitive actions such as nightly backups, log rotation, or system health checks. The secure, encrypted nature of SSH ensures that sensitive commands and their outputs remain protected during transit, even when operating over untrusted networks.

Automation becomes even more powerful when SSH is combined with key-based authentication. By configuring private-public key pairs and distributing public keys to target servers, administrators enable passwordless logins that facilitate seamless automation. Scripts and tools can authenticate automatically without human intervention, reducing friction and supporting fully automated workflows. This is particularly important when automating tasks across hundreds or thousands of servers, where manual password entry would be impractical.

SSH also plays a critical role in file synchronization and distribution tasks. Automated deployment scripts commonly use SCP or SFTP over SSH to transfer application code, configuration files, or other artifacts to remote servers. Once the necessary files are in place, SSH commands can trigger application restarts, configuration reloads, or other necessary steps to finalize the deployment. For example, a deployment script might first package a web application, then use scp to upload it to multiple servers, followed by ssh commands to restart web server processes, all without human involvement.

In large-scale environments, orchestration tools such as Ansible leverage SSH as their default transport protocol to automate configuration management and infrastructure provisioning. Ansible playbooks, written in YAML, define a series of tasks that the orchestration tool executes on target servers via SSH connections. Since Ansible operates in an agentless model, there is no need to install additional software on the remote hosts—only SSH access is required. This makes Ansible ideal for automating infrastructure across heterogeneous environments, where Linux, BSD, and other UNIX-like systems coexist.

Automated patch management is another key use case for SSH-based automation. Security teams and system administrators often use SSH-enabled scripts or orchestration platforms to automatically check for available software updates, apply patches, and reboot servers when necessary. In mission-critical environments, these automated processes ensure that systems remain up to date and protected against known vulnerabilities without relying solely on manual intervention.

Continuous integration and continuous deployment (CI/CD) pipelines also heavily rely on SSH to automate tasks across environments. Popular CI/CD tools such as Jenkins, GitLab CI, and CircleCI often use SSH to securely connect to deployment targets, where they execute build, test, and deployment steps. For instance, after passing automated tests, a pipeline may initiate an SSH session to production servers to deploy new application versions, apply infrastructure changes, or update environment variables.

Another powerful aspect of SSH automation is remote job execution. By issuing single commands or multi-line scripts over SSH, administrators can perform complex tasks directly on remote systems. These may include database queries, filesystem snapshots, or performance tuning activities. SSH enables the chaining of multiple commands, the use of environment variables, and even conditional logic within remote sessions, effectively allowing users to replicate local scripting capabilities on remote hosts.

Automation with SSH is not limited to server environments. It is also widely used in network device management, especially in environments where routers, switches, and firewalls support SSH access. Network engineers can automate device configuration backups, firmware updates, and network performance monitoring using SSH-enabled scripts or tools. This reduces the time spent on repetitive tasks while ensuring consistency across a wide range of network devices.

To further extend automation capabilities, SSH can be integrated with version control workflows. Developers often use SSH keys to securely interact with Git repositories hosted on platforms such as GitHub or GitLab. Automated scripts and pipelines leverage SSH to pull source code, push updates, or trigger repository hooks, all while maintaining secure communication channels between the build environment and the repository.

Security remains a critical consideration when automating tasks with SSH. It is essential to protect private keys used in automation workflows by storing them securely, limiting their permissions, and enforcing strong passphrases where possible. Administrators should also restrict SSH key access to specific servers or roles and periodically rotate keys to minimize exposure risks. In some environments, ephemeral keys or SSH certificates issued by a certificate authority can be used to limit the lifespan of authentication credentials, aligning with security best practices.

Logging and auditing automated SSH sessions are equally important. Automated processes should leave clear traces in system logs, enabling administrators to monitor for anomalies, investigate failed tasks, and ensure accountability. Centralized logging solutions and Security Information and Event Management (SIEM) platforms help organizations gain visibility into automated SSH activities and detect unauthorized or suspicious behavior.

SSH agent forwarding, when used carefully, can also enhance automation in multi-hop environments where intermediary jump hosts are required. By forwarding the SSH agent from the local machine through bastion hosts to target servers, automation scripts can securely authenticate across segmented networks without copying sensitive keys to intermediate systems. However, this should be paired with agent lifetime restrictions and access controls to mitigate potential security risks.

Modern DevOps practices increasingly favor combining SSH automation with containerization and cloud-native tooling. Automation scripts may leverage SSH to manage virtual machines or cloud-hosted instances while integrating with container orchestration platforms such as Kubernetes for workload management. Even in environments moving towards API-driven infrastructure management, SSH remains a trusted fallback for scenarios requiring direct, secure access to underlying systems.

SSH's flexibility, simplicity, and security have made it a core component of automation strategies in every sector, from finance and healthcare to telecommunications and technology. Its ability to streamline workflows, reduce manual labor, and enforce consistent operational practices ensures that organizations can operate at scale with confidence. By using SSH as the backbone of automated infrastructure and application management, teams can focus on innovation and problem-solving, knowing that repetitive and critical tasks are handled reliably and securely.

SSH Jump Hosts and Bastion Servers

In modern network architectures, where strict segmentation and layered security controls are critical to protecting sensitive systems, SSH jump hosts and bastion servers play a fundamental role in facilitating secure access to internal resources. As organizations move toward multi-tier environments, whether in traditional data centers or cloud deployments, direct access to internal servers is often prohibited for security and compliance reasons. Instead, users are required to first connect to an intermediary system that acts as a gatekeeper to the internal network. This intermediary system is commonly referred to as a jump host or a bastion server.

A jump host is a hardened server that serves as a single entry point into a restricted network segment. It acts as a secure intermediary through which all SSH traffic must flow before reaching internal or private servers. By funneling remote access through a single, controlled node, organizations reduce the exposure of critical assets to the public internet while maintaining centralized oversight over who can reach what. Bastion servers, a term often used interchangeably with jump hosts, follow the same principle but may have additional security functions, such as acting as an audit point or integrating with privileged access management solutions.

The primary purpose of a jump host is to provide a controlled choke point that enforces authentication, logging, and monitoring of all traffic passing through it. By isolating internal servers from direct access, organizations create a network boundary that forces users to first connect to the jump host, which typically resides within a demilitarized zone or a dedicated subnet with strict firewall rules. Once authenticated on the jump host, users can initiate subsequent SSH connections to internal servers, either manually or automatically using tools like SSH agent forwarding or ProxyJump configurations.

Implementing jump hosts significantly improves the security posture of an organization. By centralizing access through a single point, administrators can enforce uniform security policies such as multi-factor authentication (MFA), session logging, and intrusion detection. Additionally, it allows for easier application of network segmentation strategies, where critical internal servers reside in isolated private subnets inaccessible from the internet. Only the jump host has the necessary permissions to bridge these segmented networks, creating a security buffer against external threats.

Jump hosts are also an effective measure against lateral movement in the event of a compromised workstation or account. Since internal servers cannot be reached directly, attackers must first breach the jump host, which is typically hardened and closely monitored. This extra layer of defense helps slow down potential attacks, providing defenders with more time to detect and respond to intrusions.

Administrators can further harden jump hosts by minimizing installed software, disabling unnecessary services, and applying security benchmarks specific to bastion systems.

SSH configuration files play a critical role in optimizing workflows through jump hosts. By leveraging the ProxyJump directive in the ~/.ssh/config file, users can define multi-hop SSH connections that automatically route through the jump host. For example, an administrator might configure a host block specifying that all connections to internal servers within a certain subnet must route through the designated bastion server. This eliminates the need to manually log in to the jump host and then reissue SSH commands from there, improving efficiency while maintaining secure access paths.

SSH agent forwarding can be used in combination with jump hosts to avoid storing private keys on intermediary systems. When agent forwarding is enabled, the local SSH agent forwards authentication requests through the jump host, allowing users to authenticate to internal servers without copying sensitive private keys to the bastion. However, this must be used cautiously, as any process on the jump host with sufficient privileges could hijack the forwarded agent. Security best practices dictate limiting agent forwarding only to trusted bastion hosts and restricting its usage through configuration.

Some organizations extend the functionality of their bastion servers by integrating them with privileged access management (PAM) solutions. PAM platforms enhance control and monitoring by providing features such as session recording, real-time auditing, and approval workflows. Users may be required to request access to internal servers through the PAM system, which then brokers SSH sessions via the jump host. This approach provides an additional layer of security and auditability, supporting regulatory compliance requirements and internal governance policies.

Cloud environments also benefit significantly from the use of bastion hosts. In public cloud platforms like AWS, Azure, or Google Cloud, virtual machines within private subnets often lack public IP addresses for security reasons. To access these instances, administrators deploy a bastion host within a public subnet that has inbound SSH access restricted to specific IP ranges, typically corporate networks or VPNs.

From this bastion, administrators can SSH into private instances via their internal IP addresses. Cloud-native tools further enhance this model by integrating bastion hosts with security groups, IAM policies, and cloud-specific monitoring services.

High-availability configurations are another consideration for organizations relying heavily on bastion servers. To prevent a single point of failure, it is common to deploy multiple bastion hosts across different availability zones or regions. Load balancers or DNS-based routing can distribute connections across these bastion servers, ensuring resilience even if one jump host becomes unavailable. Automation tools can also be used to ensure that new bastion hosts are deployed with hardened configurations and updated with the latest security patches as part of infrastructure-as-code pipelines.

Logging and monitoring are essential aspects of managing jump hosts. Since all administrative traffic passes through the bastion, it serves as a natural audit point. Administrators should configure comprehensive logging of all SSH session activity, including user logins, commands executed, and session durations. Centralized log management solutions and SIEM platforms can collect and analyze this data for anomalies, unauthorized access attempts, and policy violations. Advanced deployments may also include session capture tools that record full terminal sessions for later review.

To further reduce the attack surface, many organizations implement just-in-time (JIT) access to bastion hosts. With JIT access, bastion hosts are normally inaccessible, and access is granted only on demand for a limited time after approval. This approach minimizes persistent exposure to the internet, limiting the time window during which the jump host can be targeted by attackers.

Despite their benefits, bastion servers and jump hosts require careful management. Misconfigurations, such as weak authentication settings, excessive user privileges, or lack of monitoring, can turn these critical access points into vulnerable targets. Regular audits, patch management, and adherence to security best practices are necessary to maintain the integrity of the jump host and the security of the network it protects.

SSH jump hosts and bastion servers remain essential components of secure network architecture, offering centralized control, enhanced security, and operational efficiency for accessing internal resources. As environments grow more complex and distributed, these systems will continue to serve as trusted gatekeepers, protecting critical assets from external threats while enabling secure and compliant remote access.

Securing SSH with Fail2Ban and Firewalls

While SSH is inherently secure due to its use of strong encryption and robust authentication mechanisms, it is still a frequent target for attackers seeking unauthorized access to servers. The ubiquity of SSH on internet-facing systems means that malicious actors regularly scan for open SSH ports and attempt brute force login attempts or exploit misconfigurations. To further harden SSH beyond its default capabilities, security professionals often rely on a layered defense strategy. Two of the most effective and complementary tools in this strategy are Fail2Ban and firewalls, which work together to reduce exposure and actively block potential threats before they can compromise a system.

Fail2Ban is an intrusion prevention system designed to detect and respond to suspicious activity by scanning log files for patterns that indicate malicious behavior. It is particularly effective at countering brute force attacks, where attackers attempt to guess SSH credentials through repeated login attempts. Once Fail2Ban detects a certain number of failed login attempts from the same IP address, it triggers an automated response, typically by adding a temporary rule to the system's firewall to block traffic from that IP address for a specified duration. This action significantly slows down or completely stops automated attack tools by cutting off their ability to make further attempts.

The beauty of Fail2Ban lies in its flexibility and extensibility. While it is most commonly used to protect SSH, Fail2Ban can also monitor logs from other services such as FTP servers, web applications, or mail servers. For SSH specifically, Fail2Ban monitors the system's authentication logs, such as /var/log/auth.log on Debian-based systems or /var/log/secure on Red Hat-based distributions, looking for entries related to failed login attempts, invalid users, or other suspicious SSH activity. The tool operates using a system of filters and actions. Filters define the patterns to look for in logs, while actions specify what to do when those patterns are detected. In the case of SSH protection, the typical action is to issue an iptables rule that blocks the offending IP address for a configurable period.

Tuning Fail2Ban's parameters is critical for balancing security and usability. By default, many installations block an IP after five failed login attempts within a short time frame, such as ten minutes. However, these thresholds can be adjusted to suit an organization's specific needs. Aggressive settings can deter persistent attackers more quickly, while more lenient settings can prevent legitimate users from being locked out due to mistyped passwords or network issues. Additionally, Fail2Ban can be configured to permanently ban repeat offenders or integrate with external notification systems to alert administrators when bans are triggered.

Firewalls play an equally vital role in securing SSH. A properly configured firewall reduces the system's attack surface by strictly controlling which IP addresses are permitted to initiate SSH connections in the first place. Many organizations implement firewall rules that restrict SSH access to known, trusted IP ranges, such as corporate networks, VPN endpoints, or specific administrative workstations. By narrowing the window of exposure, firewalls can block a majority of opportunistic attackers who scan large swaths of the internet for accessible SSH servers.

Modern firewall tools such as iptables, nftables, and firewalld on Linux systems provide fine-grained control over SSH access. Administrators can define rules that specify allowed source IP addresses, destination ports, and connection states. For example, a basic iptables rule might allow SSH traffic only from a specific subnet, dropping all other inbound SSH traffic silently. This not only prevents unauthorized users from attempting to brute force the server but also reduces log noise, as failed connection attempts from unauthorized IPs never reach the SSH daemon.

Cloud environments provide additional firewall capabilities through security groups or network access control lists (ACLs). In platforms such as AWS, Azure, or Google Cloud, security groups act as virtual firewalls at the instance level, allowing administrators to define rules that restrict SSH access to certain IP ranges or VPCs. These controls are often integrated into infrastructure-as-code workflows, ensuring that firewall policies are consistently applied to new cloud instances during automated deployments.

Fail2Ban and firewalls complement each other by addressing different layers of the security stack. Firewalls serve as the first line of defense, preventing unauthorized SSH traffic from ever reaching the server. Fail2Ban, on the other hand, acts as a dynamic, reactive measure that responds to suspicious activity from IP addresses that are otherwise allowed through the firewall. In scenarios where SSH access must be permitted from a broader range of IP addresses, such as for remote workers or globally distributed teams, Fail2Ban provides critical protection against brute force attacks that firewalls alone may not fully address.

For organizations with more complex needs, additional security measures can be integrated alongside Fail2Ban and firewalls to harden SSH further. Rate limiting with tools such as iptables' recent module or nftables' set elements can reduce the rate at which new SSH connections are accepted, further mitigating brute force attempts. Geo-blocking can also be implemented via firewalls to restrict SSH access to specific countries or regions, especially in environments where remote access is only expected from certain locations.

Fail2Ban can also be extended with custom filters and actions to tailor its behavior to unique operational requirements. For instance, administrators can configure Fail2Ban to send email alerts, trigger webhook notifications, or integrate with SIEM platforms when bans occur. This increases visibility into potential security threats and enables faster incident response. Additionally, Fail2Ban's actions can be customized to interact with cloud-native firewall APIs, enabling the automated blocking of IP addresses at the infrastructure level across multiple servers or instances.

One common best practice is to pair Fail2Ban with a non-standard SSH port. While security through obscurity should never be the sole defensive measure, moving SSH to a higher, non-default port can reduce the volume of automated scans and brute force attempts, allowing Fail2Ban to focus on more targeted threats. Coupled with robust firewall rules and dynamic bans, this practice creates multiple layers of defense that make successful exploitation significantly more difficult for attackers.

Regular testing and auditing of firewall configurations and Fail2Ban rules are essential to maintaining their effectiveness. Misconfigurations can lead to legitimate users being locked out or attackers finding gaps in the security perimeter. Periodic reviews of Fail2Ban's log files and ban lists help identify false positives, optimize settings, and refine filters for the evolving threat landscape. Similarly, firewall rule sets should be audited to ensure they are up-to-date, minimalistic, and aligned with the organization's security policies.

Securing SSH with Fail2Ban and firewalls is a practical and highly effective approach to defending remote access points against the most common and persistent threats on the internet. Together, they form a dynamic and proactive security posture that protects against brute force attacks, unauthorized access, and network reconnaissance, while allowing authorized users to safely and efficiently manage systems from remote locations. By leveraging both tools in tandem, organizations create a hardened perimeter that supports the secure and reliable operation of critical services across diverse environments.

Logging and Auditing SSH Sessions

Logging and auditing SSH sessions is an essential practice in maintaining the security, accountability, and compliance of any system where remote access is allowed. SSH serves as the primary method for administrators, developers, and automated systems to interact with servers and infrastructure, making it a high-value target for malicious actors. While SSH provides strong encryption and authentication mechanisms, these alone are insufficient to ensure the integrity and security of operations over time. Continuous monitoring through effective logging and auditing processes is crucial to detecting unauthorized access, investigating incidents, and satisfying regulatory requirements.

By default, SSH servers log various activities related to session management, including successful and failed login attempts, session closures, disconnections, and authentication failures. These logs are typically written to system log files such as /var/log/auth.log on Debian-based systems or /var/log/secure on Red Hat-based systems. These records form the foundation of SSH auditing and are invaluable for identifying trends, anomalies, and specific incidents related to remote access.

Every SSH login attempt generates entries detailing the source IP address, the username used for authentication, and whether the login was successful or denied. These basic logs serve as a first line of defense by enabling administrators to identify brute force attacks, credential stuffing attempts, or login attempts from suspicious geolocations. For example, repeated failed login attempts from the same IP address may indicate an ongoing attack, while successful logins from unexpected regions could signal a compromised account.

Beyond login attempts, detailed session logging captures additional context, such as when a session starts and ends, how long it remains active, and which commands are executed. While the default SSH logs do not record commands issued during sessions, organizations with higher security and compliance requirements often implement additional auditing tools to capture this data. Solutions such as auditd, OSSEC, or session recording tools can provide detailed visibility into user actions within an SSH session, allowing for deeper investigation and post-incident forensics.

Session auditing is critical for regulated industries such as finance, healthcare, and government, where organizations must demonstrate accountability and control over administrative actions. Regulations like PCI-DSS, HIPAA, and SOX often mandate that organizations log administrative access to systems handling sensitive data and retain these logs for a defined retention period. Failure to implement effective auditing mechanisms may result in compliance violations, financial penalties, and reputational damage.

One approach to enhancing auditing capabilities is the implementation of shell wrapper scripts or restricted shells that log user commands. This method captures every command executed within a session and logs it to a centralized location. Alternatively, modern tools such as session recording gateways can record entire SSH sessions, capturing both input and output streams. This creates a complete audit trail that can be reviewed later in the event of a security incident or compliance audit. Some solutions also provide playback functionality, allowing administrators to observe the session as if it were occurring in real-time.

Centralizing SSH logs is another best practice to ensure effective monitoring and response. Rather than storing logs solely on individual servers, organizations often forward SSH-related logs to centralized log management systems or Security Information and Event Management (SIEM) platforms. This centralization facilitates correlation across multiple systems, enabling security teams to detect patterns of suspicious activity that may go unnoticed when reviewing logs on a per-server basis. For example, simultaneous login attempts from the same IP address across several servers might indicate a coordinated attack, whereas such activity may appear innocuous in isolation.

In distributed environments, centralizing logs also helps streamline compliance reporting. Security teams can generate automated reports that demonstrate adherence to policies, such as regular account usage reviews, login trends, and anomalous access patterns. SIEM platforms often provide dashboards and automated alerting mechanisms, allowing organizations to detect suspicious SSH activity in real-time and respond quickly to potential threats.

Auditing SSH sessions also supports insider threat detection. While external attackers often dominate cybersecurity discussions, insiders with elevated privileges pose a significant risk to organizational security. By logging user commands and session activities, organizations can detect unauthorized actions such as data exfiltration, privilege escalation, or the modification of critical system files. Early detection of insider threats is crucial in minimizing potential damage and maintaining the trust of stakeholders and regulators.

To maintain the integrity of logs, it is vital to implement protections against tampering. Logs should be stored on secure, write-once or append-only media where possible, preventing unauthorized users from modifying or deleting log entries to cover their tracks. Additionally, logs can be cryptographically signed to ensure their authenticity and integrity during transport and storage. In some high-security environments, logs are forwarded in real-time to a separate, hardened logging server that is inaccessible to regular users and administrators.

Organizations operating in cloud environments must also consider the logging and auditing of SSH sessions in virtualized or containerized systems. Cloud service providers often offer native tools for log collection and monitoring. For example, AWS CloudTrail can capture API calls related to SSH key management and instance access, while AWS CloudWatch can collect system-level logs from virtual machines. These tools can be integrated into a broader centralized monitoring strategy, ensuring that remote access activities within cloud infrastructure are fully auditable.

Granular auditing policies should be enforced across all systems to define what information is logged and who has access to view or modify logs. Access to sensitive logs must be restricted to authorized personnel only, with role-based access controls implemented to prevent unauthorized viewing of potentially sensitive command outputs or administrative actions. Logs themselves may contain sensitive information, such as usernames, file paths, or command-line arguments, so care must be taken to strike a balance between effective auditing and data protection requirements.

Regular reviews and audits of SSH session logs are an essential part of maintaining a proactive security posture. Security teams should conduct periodic assessments of log data to identify gaps, unusual trends, and potential indicators of compromise. Automated tools and scripts can help streamline these reviews by flagging anomalies such as out-of-hours logins, new accounts with administrative privileges, or connections from unrecognized IP ranges.

Logging and auditing SSH sessions serve as a vital security control in any environment that relies on remote access. These practices not only support compliance but also provide the visibility necessary to detect, investigate, and respond to threats. As cyberattacks continue to grow in sophistication, a robust SSH auditing strategy ensures that organizations can quickly identify unauthorized activities, enforce accountability, and protect critical infrastructure from both external and internal risks.

The Role of SSH in DevOps

SSH plays a fundamental role in the world of DevOps, acting as a backbone for secure communication, system automation, and infrastructure management. As organizations embrace continuous integration, continuous deployment, and rapid iteration, SSH serves as a key enabler for automating tasks, configuring systems, and maintaining security across distributed environments. The nature of DevOps practices demands tools that are versatile, scriptable, and secure, and SSH provides all these capabilities, making it indispensable for modern software development and IT operations teams.

At the core of DevOps is the principle of automation. Teams aim to reduce manual intervention in the deployment and management of applications, and SSH is often integrated directly into scripts and automation frameworks to facilitate these processes. With SSH, DevOps engineers can remotely execute commands, synchronize files, and manage services on multiple servers simultaneously, all within a secure and encrypted session. SSH allows these operations to be performed in an unattended fashion, often combined with key-based authentication to enable passwordless logins in automated workflows.

One of the primary use cases of SSH in DevOps is infrastructure provisioning and configuration management. Tools such as Ansible, one of the most widely adopted DevOps tools, rely on SSH as their default transport layer to push configurations and execute tasks on remote nodes. Because Ansible operates agentlessly, it uses SSH to connect to target systems and perform actions such as installing packages, configuring services, and deploying applications. This allows DevOps teams to maintain infrastructure as code, where entire system configurations are defined in version-controlled playbooks that can be applied automatically across environments via SSH connections.

SSH also plays a crucial role in the orchestration of deployment pipelines. Continuous deployment workflows require that applications and services are delivered to production environments frequently and reliably. SSH is frequently used to automate the deployment of application builds from CI/CD platforms like Jenkins, GitLab CI, or CircleCI to staging or production servers. A typical pipeline may involve an automated script that packages an application, uploads it to remote servers using SCP or SFTP over SSH, and executes commands to stop services, deploy updates, and restart applications. By doing so securely through SSH, organizations ensure that sensitive information and deployment processes remain protected, even when interacting with servers across untrusted networks.

In addition to deployment tasks, SSH is commonly used for remote monitoring and health checks of production systems. Automated scripts or monitoring tools often establish SSH connections to run diagnostic commands, collect performance metrics, and check service statuses. This information feeds into dashboards, alerting systems, and automated incident response mechanisms that form the backbone of modern DevOps monitoring strategies. SSH's ability to securely tunnel this information makes it a preferred choice for operations teams that need to continuously assess the state of remote infrastructure.

Another critical aspect of SSH in DevOps is its integration with version control systems. Platforms such as GitHub, GitLab, and Bitbucket support SSH for secure authentication when interacting with repositories. Developers and automation tools rely on SSH keys to clone repositories, push code changes, and trigger automated builds, ensuring that source code and related assets are transmitted securely. SSH keys can be configured with limited permissions, such as read-only access, enhancing security in collaborative environments.

DevOps teams also frequently use SSH tunneling to securely bridge services across different networks. In hybrid cloud or multi-cloud environments, internal services such as databases or application programming interfaces (APIs) may not be directly exposed to the public internet. SSH tunnels allow developers and automation tools to securely forward ports from local machines to remote services, providing temporary, encrypted access during development or deployment activities. This practice not only enhances security but also supports network segmentation and micro-segmentation strategies critical to modern cloud-native architectures.

For teams managing Kubernetes or containerized environments, SSH remains important for node-level access and troubleshooting. While container orchestration platforms abstract much of the infrastructure management, there are times when DevOps engineers must SSH into worker nodes to resolve low-level system issues, adjust network configurations, or debug resource constraints. Additionally, SSH is sometimes used in conjunction with kubectl, Helm, or other Kubernetes tools during the deployment or scaling of microservices, particularly when working with on-premises clusters or custom cloud deployments.

In serverless or fully managed cloud environments, SSH's role is reduced, but it remains essential for connecting to bastion hosts or intermediary jump servers that provide access to more restricted internal networks. DevOps teams rely on SSH bastion hosts to securely manage resources in private subnets, perform audits, and deploy code to servers that are isolated from direct internet exposure. SSH agent forwarding can be used in conjunction with bastions to allow seamless multi-hop access without storing private keys on intermediate systems.

The flexibility of SSH also supports DevOps practices that involve disaster recovery and business continuity planning. Automated backup scripts often use SSH to securely transfer database dumps, configuration files, and application data to off-site or cloud-based backup servers. In the event of a failure or disaster scenario, these same SSH-powered workflows can automate recovery processes, including restoring systems, reapplying infrastructure configurations, and redeploying applications, ensuring minimal downtime.

Security is a constant concern in DevOps workflows, and SSH contributes by enabling secure access controls and encrypted communications. DevOps teams use SSH key-based authentication with strict key management policies to limit access to critical infrastructure. Short-lived SSH certificates issued by internal certificate authorities are increasingly popular in environments where SSH keys must be rotated frequently, and temporary access is preferable to persistent credentials. This aligns well with zero trust security principles, where access to systems is continuously verified and short-lived.

As infrastructure grows in scale and complexity, SSH's role in DevOps continues to evolve. Many organizations now integrate SSH usage with secrets management systems and privileged access management solutions. These integrations automate the secure retrieval of SSH keys or certificates when needed, reduce the risk of key sprawl, and provide audit trails for every SSH session initiated as part of automated workflows.

In highly dynamic environments, DevOps engineers also rely on SSH in combination with dynamic inventory management. Tools like Ansible's dynamic inventory plugins query cloud APIs to discover active infrastructure and automatically configure SSH connections to these hosts, reducing the manual effort needed to keep track of constantly changing resources. This capability is essential in environments that use autoscaling groups, ephemeral instances, or container clusters, where hosts may appear and disappear rapidly based on workload demands.

SSH continues to be a core component of DevOps toolchains, providing secure, reliable, and flexible access to systems across diverse environments. It empowers teams to automate repetitive tasks, maintain continuous delivery pipelines, and ensure secure operations across development, staging, and production environments. As DevOps practices advance and organizations increasingly adopt hybrid and cloud-native models, SSH remains a critical enabler of secure and efficient infrastructure and application management.

SSH in Zero Trust Architectures

SSH remains one of the most trusted and widely used tools for secure remote access and system management, but the rise of zero trust architectures has prompted a reevaluation of how SSH is implemented and controlled in modern environments. Zero trust is a security framework that operates on the principle of never implicitly trusting any user, system, or network—regardless of whether they are inside or outside the organization's perimeter. Instead, zero trust demands continuous verification of every access request, strict segmentation of resources, and minimal privilege allocation. As organizations adopt zero trust models, SSH must evolve from being a simple remote access tool to becoming an integrated part of a dynamic and heavily monitored security ecosystem.

In traditional network architectures, SSH is often used under the assumption that once a user or device is inside the corporate network, their access to internal systems is implicitly trusted. However, in zero trust environments, this perimeter-based thinking is replaced with a model where every request, even from within the internal network, must be explicitly authenticated and authorized. SSH, therefore, plays a dual role in this model: it continues to provide secure, encrypted remote access, but it must also conform to the principles of least privilege, continuous authentication, and rigorous auditing.

One of the key adaptations of SSH within zero trust architectures is the integration of identity-aware access controls. Rather than relying solely on static SSH keys or long-lived credentials, zero trust models often incorporate centralized identity providers and short-lived credentials into their workflows. SSH access may be brokered by identity-aware proxies or certificate authorities that issue time-bound certificates based on real-time policy evaluations. These policies consider factors such as user identity, device posture, location, and the sensitivity of the target resource before issuing access credentials. By limiting the lifetime of SSH credentials to a short window, organizations reduce the risk of key compromise and align with zero trust principles of dynamic access.

SSH certificate authorities (CAs) are particularly well-suited to this model. Instead of deploying static public keys to every server, administrators configure servers to trust the CA, which issues short-lived certificates to users after successful identity verification and policy checks. This enables just-in-time access to specific resources, ensuring that no user has perpetual access to any system. Moreover, these certificates can include metadata that defines access scope, such as which servers the user may access and which commands they are authorized to run. This supports the enforcement of granular, context-aware policies aligned with zero trust methodologies.

Micro-segmentation is another pillar of zero trust architectures, and SSH plays a vital role in enforcing it. In micro-segmented networks, resources are broken down into small, isolated zones with strict controls over how users and services communicate across boundaries. SSH traffic must be carefully routed through designated bastion hosts or jump servers, each tightly controlled by access policies and network segmentation rules. Unlike traditional bastion hosts, which may allow broad access to internal networks, zero trust bastion hosts limit connections to predefined resource groups, with user access strictly governed by dynamic policies.

In zero trust environments, the deployment of SSH gateways and identity-aware proxies further strengthens the security model. These gateways act as enforcement points, mediating all SSH traffic and applying contextual access controls. They integrate with single sign-on (SSO) solutions, multi-factor authentication (MFA), and device posture checks to verify that every access request adheres to corporate security policies. For example, a developer attempting to access a production server through SSH may be required to authenticate using SSO credentials and complete an MFA challenge, while the proxy ensures that the request originates from a compliant, managed device.

Continuous monitoring and auditing of SSH activity are essential to maintaining visibility and trust in a zero trust environment. Traditional logging mechanisms are augmented with advanced session recording, full command auditing, and real-time behavioral analytics. Every SSH session, including keystrokes, file transfers, and system interactions, is recorded and correlated with the user's identity and access context. This provides security teams with deep insights into user activity and enables rapid investigation of anomalies or policy violations. Security information and event management (SIEM) platforms consume this data, applying machine learning and threat intelligence to detect suspicious patterns and potential breaches.

Automation also plays a critical role in aligning SSH usage with zero trust objectives. Modern zero trust platforms integrate with infrastructure-as-code (IaC) tools and configuration management systems to automate the deployment of tightly controlled SSH configurations across diverse environments. Automated processes ensure that SSH servers disable insecure protocols, restrict root login, enforce key rotation policies, and apply IP whitelisting where appropriate. This reduces the risk of human error and enforces consistent security baselines across all systems.

SSH tunneling and port forwarding are additional considerations within zero trust models. While SSH tunnels are a powerful tool for securing data in transit, they can also be exploited to bypass network segmentation controls if left unchecked. Zero trust architectures typically limit or entirely disable SSH port forwarding except where explicitly required. When allowed, forwarding is often brokered through secure proxies that inspect and control the traffic within the tunnel, ensuring that only approved services and destinations are reachable.

Zero trust principles also dictate that SSH access be continuously reevaluated, rather than granted on a static, role-based model. Modern implementations integrate with policy engines that assess context in real-time. Factors such as changes in user behavior, network anomalies, or new threat intelligence can trigger dynamic access revocation or force re-authentication during active SSH sessions. This adaptive approach minimizes risk by ensuring that trust is never assumed and that every session remains subject to policy enforcement.

In cloud and hybrid environments, where workloads are distributed across multiple providers and regions, SSH in zero trust models must extend across these boundaries without compromising security. Centralized identity providers and access proxies can act as federated control points, enforcing zero trust policies consistently across on-premises and cloud-hosted systems. This unification ensures that users accessing virtual machines, containers, or serverless workloads adhere to the same stringent authentication, authorization, and auditing requirements, regardless of where the resource resides.

SSH remains indispensable within zero trust architectures but requires a shift from traditional usage patterns. It must be tightly integrated with identity, access management, and security controls to meet the continuous verification demands of a zero trust model. When correctly implemented, SSH serves as a secure, auditable, and context-aware access mechanism that supports the principles of zero trust while preserving the flexibility and power that make it a cornerstone of modern infrastructure management.

Multiplexing and Reusing SSH Connections

SSH is widely known for enabling secure remote access to servers, but one of its lesser-known yet highly valuable features is its ability to multiplex and reuse connections. In environments where users frequently establish multiple SSH sessions to the same server, multiplexing allows for more efficient and faster connections by reusing an existing secure channel. This feature is especially beneficial for system administrators, developers, and automated scripts that need to execute multiple remote commands or file transfers in rapid succession.

Without multiplexing, every new SSH session initiates a full handshake process, including negotiating encryption algorithms, performing key exchanges, and authenticating the user. While this handshake is secure and efficient, it still introduces a small but cumulative overhead, especially noticeable when executing many SSH commands in quick succession. In scenarios where users frequently SSH into the same server or run automated scripts that trigger multiple SSH commands, these repeated handshakes can add up, leading to delays and unnecessary consumption of system and network resources.

SSH multiplexing addresses this issue by creating a master connection to the target server, which subsequent sessions can piggyback on. Once the master connection is established, additional sessions to the same server reuse the existing encrypted channel, bypassing the full handshake process. This drastically reduces the time it takes to establish new connections, as the authentication and cryptographic negotiations are only performed once during the creation of the master session.

This behavior is controlled using the ControlMaster, ControlPath, and ControlPersist options in the SSH client configuration. ControlMaster enables or disables multiplexing, ControlPath defines the location of the Unix domain socket that will be used for communication between the master and subsequent sessions, and ControlPersist controls how long the master connection should remain open after the last client session terminates.

When configured properly, SSH multiplexing becomes nearly invisible to the user. For example, a user connecting to a remote server using ssh user@host with multiplexing enabled will create the initial master connection. Any subsequent ssh commands to the same server within the lifespan of that master connection will instantly reuse it, significantly reducing connection latency. This is especially valuable when executing short-lived commands, such as retrieving system information, modifying configurations, or performing file operations remotely.

In practice, administrators and developers can configure multiplexing globally in the ~/.ssh/config file. By adding a block such as Host *, ControlMaster auto, ControlPath ~/.ssh/sockets/%r@%h:%p, and ControlPersist 10m, the SSH client will automatically create and reuse a master connection for any host it connects to. The ControlPersist directive ensures that the master connection remains open for ten minutes after the last related session ends, allowing users to benefit from multiplexing without having to manually manage the lifecycle of the master session.

The benefits of multiplexing extend beyond interactive sessions. Automated scripts, CI/CD pipelines, and orchestration tools that rely on SSH can execute multiple remote commands much faster when multiplexing is enabled. For instance, a deployment script that copies files to a remote server using SCP and then runs a series of remote commands via SSH will complete significantly faster, as each command or file transfer will reuse the master connection rather than creating a new SSH session each time.

Multiplexing also reduces the computational load on both the client and server. Since key exchange and encryption negotiation are computationally intensive, reusing a connection means these processes are only executed once per master session, freeing up system resources for other tasks. This can be particularly advantageous in resource-constrained environments, such as embedded systems, IoT devices, or virtual machines with limited CPU capacity.

While multiplexing is highly beneficial, it does introduce some operational considerations. For example, the master connection is typically associated with a Unix domain socket file located on the client machine. If this socket is deleted or becomes inaccessible, new client sessions will revert to creating fresh SSH connections without reusing the existing channel. Therefore, administrators often specify a dedicated directory such as ~/.ssh/sockets to store these socket files and ensure it has the proper permissions.

Additionally, multiplexing can complicate session management in some cases. When ControlPersist is used, the master connection can linger even after the user has finished working on the remote server. While this can improve efficiency for follow-up tasks, it may also leave idle open connections that could potentially be exploited if the client device is compromised. To mitigate this, organizations often set conservative ControlPersist timers and rely on tools like SSH's ServerAliveInterval option to automatically terminate stale sessions.

Security best practices must still be observed when using multiplexing. The underlying SSH connection still adheres to the authentication and encryption settings defined by the server and client. However, multiplexed sessions should only be used on trusted networks and endpoints. For sensitive environments, additional controls such as IP whitelisting, multi-factor authentication, and host-based firewall rules should be used to reduce the risks associated with leaving master connections open for extended periods.

Multiplexing can also be combined with other SSH features, such as agent forwarding and port forwarding, to create powerful workflows. For example, a developer working on a private Git repository hosted on an internal server may set up an SSH tunnel and forward ports over a multiplexed connection, all while maintaining agent forwarding to sign Git commits securely. By reusing the master connection, these operations happen seamlessly without the latency associated with setting up new SSH sessions for each task.

In clustered environments or during parallel operations, multiplexing provides additional efficiency. Tools like GNU parallel, Fabric, or custom bash loops that execute SSH commands across many servers in rapid succession can benefit greatly from multiplexing. Although each target server will require its own master connection, the overhead of repeated handshakes to each server is minimized, speeding up operations such as rolling deployments, log collection, or remote orchestration tasks.

Multiplexing and reusing SSH connections is a powerful yet underutilized capability that can greatly improve the performance, efficiency, and scalability of remote access workflows. By reducing connection times, lowering resource consumption, and streamlining command execution, SSH multiplexing allows teams to operate more effectively in fast-paced environments where speed and reliability are critical. Whether used for day-to-day administration, automated pipelines, or complex orchestration tasks, multiplexing ensures that SSH sessions remain agile and responsive, even at scale.

SSH and IoT: Connecting to the Edge

SSH has long been a foundational tool for securing remote access to servers and devices, but its role has expanded significantly with the rise of the Internet of Things (IoT). As organizations deploy thousands or even millions of connected devices at the edge of networks, from industrial sensors to smart appliances and embedded systems, SSH serves as a critical technology for securely managing and maintaining these distributed assets. The ability to remotely access, configure, and monitor IoT devices over encrypted connections is vital in environments where physical access is impractical or impossible.

IoT devices deployed at the edge often operate in isolated or resource-constrained environments. These devices may reside in remote industrial facilities, power plants, agricultural fields, transportation networks, or even in consumer homes. Despite their diverse applications, these devices share common requirements: they must be secure, reliable, and manageable from a distance. SSH enables administrators and engineers to fulfill these requirements by providing a secure channel for device administration, diagnostics, and updates without the risk of exposing sensitive data to the open internet.

The lightweight nature of SSH makes it particularly suited for IoT ecosystems. Many IoT devices run stripped-down versions of Linux or other embedded operating systems that support minimal footprints. Even with limited CPU, memory, and storage resources, most devices can still run an SSH server. This allows organizations to deploy devices at scale while retaining the ability to manage them securely. Once SSH is enabled, administrators can remotely log in, perform system diagnostics, adjust configurations, and apply patches, reducing the need for costly and time-consuming on-site interventions.

One of the primary use cases for SSH in IoT is device provisioning and onboarding. As new devices are brought online, they often require initial configuration to connect to networks, authenticate to cloud services, and establish baseline security policies. SSH facilitates this process by allowing administrators to remotely configure these settings securely. Automation tools and scripts can leverage SSH to configure network parameters, set up VPN connections, or install necessary software components across thousands of edge devices simultaneously. In environments such as smart factories or connected vehicle fleets, where rapid and consistent onboarding is critical, SSH accelerates the deployment process.

Ongoing maintenance and software updates are another area where SSH plays a crucial role. IoT devices often operate in dynamic environments where software vulnerabilities and configuration issues must be addressed promptly. Through SSH, organizations can remotely apply patches, upgrade firmware, and adjust system settings. These updates are delivered over encrypted channels, protecting against man-in-the-middle attacks and ensuring the integrity of critical software components. Automated scripts that utilize SSH are frequently used to roll out updates to devices in batches, reducing the potential impact of bugs or downtime.

SSH also supports secure file transfers using protocols like SCP and SFTP, enabling administrators to move configuration files, logs, and diagnostic data between devices and central management servers. For example, edge devices collecting environmental or operational data can securely transmit log files to a cloud platform for further analysis. Conversely, updated AI models or machine learning algorithms can be distributed to edge devices via SSH-based transfers, enabling them to adapt to evolving business requirements or environmental conditions.

The security of IoT devices is a persistent concern, especially given the increasing prevalence of attacks targeting poorly secured devices. SSH provides a secure alternative to legacy remote management protocols that may lack encryption or robust authentication mechanisms. By enforcing strong SSH key-based authentication, organizations can prevent unauthorized access to edge devices, even if these devices are exposed to hostile networks or untrusted intermediaries. Additionally, SSH allows for the disabling of password-based logins, mitigating the risk of brute force attacks and credential stuffing.

SSH's port forwarding capabilities are especially useful in IoT environments where devices are placed behind firewalls or NAT gateways. Many IoT devices operate in networks where inbound traffic is restricted, but they can establish outbound SSH tunnels to trusted servers. By using reverse SSH tunnels, these devices can enable remote administrators to securely connect back into them from central locations. This technique is widely used in scenarios such as smart grid infrastructure, where utility companies must remotely manage substations and smart meters without exposing them directly to the internet.

IoT devices often need to integrate with cloud services to exchange data, receive commands, or report metrics. SSH enables secure communication between edge devices and cloud-hosted applications. For instance, SSH tunnels can be used to securely transmit telemetry data from field-deployed sensors to cloud-based analytics platforms. In addition, SSH serves as a reliable fallback mechanism when other forms of connectivity or device management agents fail. Administrators can leverage SSH to re-establish control of devices, diagnose network issues, and restore connectivity without requiring physical access.

Automation is key to managing IoT fleets, and SSH is commonly integrated into orchestration tools and custom scripts that facilitate large-scale device operations. Infrastructure-as-code principles are increasingly applied to edge devices, where configuration management platforms such as Ansible or SaltStack leverage SSH to push consistent configurations across diverse device types and geographies. In manufacturing plants, for example, SSH may be used to deploy software updates to thousands of programmable logic controllers (PLCs) or human-machine interface (HMI) panels as part of routine maintenance.

SSH's role in IoT is not limited to technical operations but also extends to regulatory compliance and auditing. In industries such as healthcare, energy, and transportation, compliance frameworks often mandate detailed logging of administrative actions on networked systems. By using SSH, organizations can generate logs of all remote access sessions, recording who connected to which device, when, and what actions were performed. These logs can be centralized and integrated into Security Information and Event Management (SIEM) platforms, providing audit trails that support compliance with regulatory requirements such as HIPAA, NERC CIP, or ISO/IEC 27001.

In edge computing scenarios, where data is processed locally on IoT devices before being transmitted to the cloud, SSH supports direct intervention on the compute nodes themselves. Edge devices acting as local servers, gateways, or mini data centers can be administered via SSH to tune processing workloads, deploy software containers, or optimize system performance. This capability is especially valuable when edge devices operate in bandwidth-constrained or intermittent connectivity environments, as it allows remote administrators to make critical adjustments without relying on cloud APIs.

SSH's adaptability, security, and lightweight nature make it a cornerstone technology for connecting and managing IoT devices at the edge. As organizations continue to expand their IoT deployments across industries, SSH will remain a critical tool for enabling secure, reliable, and efficient remote management of the growing network of connected devices that underpin modern business and industrial operations.

Best Practices for SSH Key Rotation

SSH key rotation is a critical security practice that organizations must implement to ensure the ongoing protection of their remote access infrastructure. SSH keys, like any form of credential, can become compromised or outdated over time, and without proper rotation processes in place, organizations risk unauthorized access, insider threats, and compliance violations. Managing SSH keys effectively requires a balance between operational efficiency and robust security policies, especially in environments where thousands of keys may be deployed across numerous systems and users.

The first step in effective SSH key rotation is establishing a formal policy that defines when and how keys should be rotated. Key rotation policies typically specify a maximum key lifetime, after which keys must be replaced. Many organizations mandate rotating keys every 90 or 180 days, while others base their schedules on the sensitivity of the systems being accessed. High-risk systems, such as production servers handling sensitive data, often require more frequent rotations compared to lower-risk environments like development sandboxes.

A common pitfall is allowing SSH keys to remain in use indefinitely without periodic review or replacement. This creates a situation where old keys may still provide access long after the user or system that created them has been decommissioned. Stale keys are particularly dangerous in organizations with high employee turnover or frequent changes in contractor and vendor access. An effective key rotation process helps eliminate these orphaned keys, reducing the overall attack surface.

Automation is essential when managing key rotation at scale. Manual processes quickly become impractical in large environments where keys are deployed across hundreds or thousands of servers. Organizations should leverage configuration management tools such as Ansible, Puppet, or SaltStack to automate the distribution of new public keys to target systems and the removal of outdated ones. These tools integrate with version control systems and CI/CD pipelines to ensure that key rotation becomes part of standard infrastructure deployment and maintenance workflows.

The rotation process typically starts with generating a new key pair for each user or system requiring access. Best practices dictate that keys be generated using secure, modern algorithms, such as Ed25519 or RSA with a minimum key length of 4096 bits. Private keys must be securely stored on the originating client machine and, where possible, protected with strong passphrases. The new public key is then distributed to the appropriate servers and added to the authorized_keys file of the relevant accounts.

It is important to overlap the validity of the old and new keys temporarily. During the transition period, both keys should be valid to avoid disrupting access to critical systems. This allows users to verify the functionality of the new key before the old key is revoked. Once the new key is confirmed operational, the old key should be promptly removed from all systems. Automating this process helps enforce consistency and ensures that no old keys are inadvertently left behind.

Key rotation also applies to service accounts and automated systems that perform unattended tasks using SSH. These accounts often lack human operators, making key rotation particularly challenging. In such cases, organizations can implement centralized secrets management solutions, such as HashiCorp Vault or AWS Secrets Manager, to manage and rotate keys or certificates programmatically. These tools offer API-driven workflows for securely delivering new keys to systems as needed while automatically deactivating old ones.

Logging and auditing are critical components of a secure key rotation strategy. Organizations should maintain detailed records of key creation, distribution, rotation, and revocation events. These logs help ensure accountability and provide evidence of compliance with security policies and regulatory requirements. Regular audits should be conducted to review key usage, validate that rotation policies are being followed, and identify any deviations from established best practices.

In environments where SSH certificates are used instead of static keys, rotation is inherently built into the system, as certificates have short expiration times by design. However, the underlying signing keys of the certificate authority (CA) still require regular rotation to maintain the security of the overall system. Organizations using SSH certificates should establish separate rotation schedules for CA keys and user or host certificates to ensure end-to-end security.

Communicating key rotation policies clearly to all users is essential. Developers, administrators, and third-party vendors must understand the importance of key rotation and their role in the process. Organizations should provide documentation and training to ensure that all stakeholders follow secure key generation and storage practices. This includes educating users on protecting their private keys, avoiding insecure storage practices, and immediately reporting lost or compromised keys.

Key rotation must also account for disaster recovery and business continuity. Backup and recovery plans should include procedures for restoring keys and re-establishing secure access to critical systems in the event of key management system failures or major incidents. Secure key escrow mechanisms, where encrypted copies of private keys are stored in a trusted location, can help facilitate rapid recovery while maintaining security controls.

Finally, organizations should integrate SSH key rotation with broader identity and access management (IAM) frameworks. By linking key management processes to IAM policies and workflows, organizations can automate the provisioning and deprovisioning of SSH keys in response to user lifecycle events. For example, when an employee leaves the company or a contractor engagement ends, associated SSH keys should be automatically revoked across all relevant systems as part of the offboarding process.

Rotating SSH keys regularly helps organizations maintain strong security postures, reduce risk exposure, and support regulatory compliance. While key rotation introduces some operational complexity, modern tools and automation platforms make it feasible to implement secure, scalable rotation processes across diverse IT environments. By embedding key rotation into daily workflows and aligning it with comprehensive security policies, organizations can significantly reduce the likelihood of unauthorized access and improve the resilience of their infrastructure.

Threats and Vulnerabilities in SSH

While SSH is regarded as one of the most secure remote access protocols available, it is not immune to threats and vulnerabilities. Its widespread adoption in securing server communications, automating workflows, and providing encrypted tunnels makes it a frequent target for attackers seeking to compromise systems. Understanding the most common risks associated with SSH is essential for maintaining a hardened security posture and defending against misuse and exploitation. Threats to SSH can stem from misconfigurations, poor key management, weak user practices, and sophisticated attack techniques that target both client and server components.

One of the most prevalent risks associated with SSH is brute force attacks. Attackers routinely scan the internet for servers with open SSH ports and attempt to guess login credentials by trying thousands of username and password combinations. Despite SSH's strong encryption, if weak or default passwords are used, brute force attacks can still be effective. Servers exposed to the internet and lacking additional protective measures such as fail2ban, IP whitelisting, or multi-factor authentication are especially vulnerable to this type of attack.

Another critical vulnerability is related to poor key management practices. SSH keys, when improperly managed, can become a significant security liability. Static keys left unrotated for long periods or shared among multiple users increase the risk of key compromise. Orphaned keys, where public keys remain authorized on servers long after the user or system that created them has been decommissioned, are a common oversight. Attackers who gain access to a lost or improperly secured private key can bypass password-based authentication altogether. Without a formal key rotation and auditing process in place, organizations may unknowingly provide persistent backdoors into critical infrastructure.

SSH agent hijacking is another threat that primarily affects environments where agent forwarding is enabled. In this scenario, when a user forwards their SSH agent through a jump host or intermediary server, any user or process with elevated privileges on that server can potentially hijack the forwarded agent to initiate connections to other systems where the user's key is trusted. This allows an attacker to impersonate the user on other trusted systems, bypassing access controls and escalating the attack laterally across the network. While agent forwarding is a convenience feature, if misused or left unrestricted, it can become a significant risk in multi-hop SSH workflows.

Man-in-the-middle (MITM) attacks are a theoretical concern when SSH host key verification is not strictly enforced. SSH relies on trust-on-first-use (TOFU), where the client accepts the server's host key the first time it connects. If an attacker is positioned between the client and server during this initial connection, they could present a rogue host key and intercept communications. While SSH encrypts traffic after the handshake, trusting a malicious host key opens the door to persistent MITM attacks. Organizations that do not manage their known_hosts files carefully or that accept changed host keys without verification are especially susceptible to this vector.

Another category of threat relates to SSH tunneling and port forwarding misuse. SSH's ability to tunnel arbitrary TCP connections can be leveraged by insiders or attackers to bypass firewalls, security controls, and network segmentation. For example, an attacker with SSH access to a compromised system could use port forwarding to access internal applications, databases, or control panels that would otherwise be inaccessible from the outside. This makes SSH a potential conduit for lateral movement inside a network, especially when combined with poor network segmentation and a lack of monitoring of internal traffic.

Vulnerabilities can also arise from outdated SSH server or client software. Like any software, OpenSSH and other SSH implementations occasionally have security vulnerabilities disclosed and patched by their maintainers. Failing to keep systems updated can leave them exposed to known exploits, such as buffer overflows, memory corruption, or other remote code execution vulnerabilities. Historically, while SSH has had relatively few critical vulnerabilities compared to other protocols, incidents like the OpenSSH vulnerability CVE-2016-0777, which exposed sensitive private keys due to information leakage via roaming feature, highlight the importance of staying current with software updates.

Misconfigured SSH servers present yet another layer of risk. Common misconfigurations include enabling root login, using outdated or weak cryptographic algorithms, failing to restrict access via firewalls, or allowing unrestricted password authentication. Permitting root login over SSH gives attackers a single, powerful target to exploit. Weak ciphers such as deprecated 3DES or low-bit RSA keys, if still allowed on a server, can weaken the confidentiality of SSH sessions. Best practices dictate configuring SSH to disable legacy algorithms, enforce key-based authentication, and prohibit direct root logins by requiring users to elevate privileges after connecting.

Insider threats are another dimension of SSH risk that organizations must address. Administrators or employees with legitimate SSH access to servers can intentionally or unintentionally misuse their privileges. Without proper monitoring, logging, and least-privilege enforcement, malicious insiders can exfiltrate sensitive data, introduce malware, or sabotage systems through SSH sessions. Additionally, insiders may create unauthorized SSH tunnels to external destinations, facilitating data leaks or external command-and-control channels.

Supply chain risks also impact SSH when SSH keys or configurations are included in development and deployment pipelines. Developers may inadvertently commit private keys or hard-coded credentials to source code repositories, making them discoverable to anyone with access to the repository. Attackers actively search public repositories for exposed SSH keys, which can be used to compromise systems if the corresponding public keys remain authorized on production servers.

The increasing adoption of cloud environments introduces new complexities in managing SSH-related risks. Cloud instances often come preconfigured with public keys injected during provisioning, but if access to the cloud console or infrastructure-as-code templates is compromised, attackers could modify key configurations or gain access through stolen automation credentials. Furthermore, cloud-native services that rely on SSH for secure communication between microservices or hybrid environments are also exposed to many of the same risks present in traditional infrastructures.

Ultimately, the security of SSH depends not only on the protocol itself but also on the policies, configurations, and practices implemented by organizations. Without proper key lifecycle management, strict configuration hardening, vigilant monitoring, and ongoing user education, even the most secure protocols can become an avenue for attack. As attackers grow more sophisticated and environments more distributed, addressing threats and vulnerabilities in SSH must be an ongoing priority, requiring continuous assessment and adaptation to emerging risks.

Hardening SSH Configurations

Hardening SSH configurations is a critical step in reducing the attack surface of servers and protecting them from unauthorized access. While SSH is inherently secure due to its robust encryption and authentication mechanisms, default configurations often leave unnecessary features enabled or allow broader access than required. By systematically reviewing and tightening SSH settings, organizations can greatly enhance their overall security posture and mitigate a wide range of common threats.

One of the most effective measures in hardening SSH is disabling password-based authentication. Passwords are often weak, reused, or susceptible to brute-force attacks. By enforcing key-based authentication, where users authenticate using cryptographic key pairs, administrators significantly reduce the likelihood of credential compromise. SSH keys are inherently stronger than passwords due to their length and complexity, and they eliminate the possibility of online brute force guessing. The relevant setting in the SSH server configuration file is PasswordAuthentication no, which ensures that only users with valid private keys can establish a session.

Another critical step is to disable root login over SSH. Allowing direct remote access to the root account exposes the most privileged user on the system to attack. Instead, users should log in with unprivileged accounts and use privilege escalation tools like sudo when administrative access is necessary. This approach not only limits exposure but also creates more granular audit trails, as actions performed via sudo are logged with the initiating user's identity. To enforce this policy, administrators should set PermitRootLogin no in the sshd_config file.

Restricting which users can initiate SSH sessions to the server is another key component of a hardened setup. By default, SSH may allow any user account on the system to attempt authentication. This can be limited by specifying AllowUsers or AllowGroups directives in the SSH configuration. For example, defining AllowUsers admin1 admin2 restricts SSH access to only the specified accounts, reducing the number of potential targets and simplifying access control.

Limiting access based on IP addresses is a widely recommended practice. Firewalls or host-based access controls can enforce network-level restrictions to ensure that only trusted IP ranges or VPN endpoints are allowed to connect to the SSH service. For example, administrators can configure iptables or firewalld to permit SSH traffic exclusively from known office networks, administrative workstations, or secure jump hosts, reducing the exposure of the SSH port to the internet.

SSH hardening also involves carefully selecting the cryptographic algorithms in use. While SSH supports a range of encryption algorithms, message authentication codes (MACs), and key exchange methods, some older algorithms may be considered weak or deprecated. The sshd_config file should specify strong, modern algorithms by setting the Ciphers, MACs, and KexAlgorithms directives. For instance, administrators may opt to allow only algorithms like aes256-gcm@openssh.com or chacha20-poly1305@openssh.com for encryption, along with SHA-2 based MACs such as hmac-sha2-512. Disabling legacy algorithms reduces the risk of downgrade attacks or vulnerabilities related to weaker cryptographic primitives.

Idle session timeout policies are also important for hardening SSH. Users may inadvertently leave sessions open, exposing them to session hijacking risks if an attacker gains access to an unattended workstation or compromised client system. The ClientAliveInterval and ClientAliveCountMax settings can be used to configure automatic disconnection of idle sessions. For example, setting ClientAliveInterval

300 and ClientAliveCountMax 0 will disconnect idle sessions after five minutes of inactivity.

Another often overlooked setting is the SSH port itself. While changing the default port from 22 to a non-standard port does not provide real security against determined attackers, it does reduce the volume of automated scans and brute force attempts that typically target port 22. In combination with other hardening techniques, this can reduce log noise and help focus attention on more significant threats.

Enabling logging and auditing within SSH is critical for tracking access and identifying anomalous behavior. SSH should be configured to log at a verbose level by setting LogLevel VERBOSE in the sshd_config file. This ensures that additional details about connection attempts, authentication methods, and session events are recorded. These logs should be monitored regularly and forwarded to centralized logging systems or SIEM platforms to enable correlation and alerting across multiple systems.

Some environments may benefit from enabling two-factor authentication (2FA) for SSH. Integrating SSH with time-based one-time password (TOTP) systems or hardware security keys adds an extra layer of protection against credential compromise. This can be implemented via PAM (Pluggable Authentication Modules) or by integrating with external identity providers that enforce multi-factor authentication.

Chroot jails and restricted shells are additional hardening measures for users who require limited access. Chroot jails restrict a user's environment to a specified directory tree, preventing them from navigating the broader file system or accessing critical system resources. Restricted shells, such as rbash or custom scripts, can further control which commands a user is permitted to execute within their session. These techniques are especially useful in environments where SSH access must be provided to third-party vendors, temporary contractors, or automated systems.

Administrators should also disable unnecessary features, such as X11 forwarding and SSH agent forwarding, unless explicitly required. X11 forwarding allows remote users to run graphical applications on their local machine through the SSH connection, which may introduce additional security risks if not properly controlled. Agent forwarding, while convenient, can expose the user's SSH agent to the remote server, increasing the risk of credential hijacking. These options can be disabled by setting X11Forwarding no and AllowAgentForwarding no in the sshd_config file.

Finally, regular security audits and vulnerability assessments should be conducted to verify the effectiveness of SSH hardening efforts. Tools like Lynis, OpenSCAP, and CIS Benchmarks can help identify misconfigurations, weak policies, or deviations from industry best practices. Hardening is not a one-time task but a continuous process that requires review and adaptation as new threats and technologies emerge.

By applying these hardening measures consistently across all systems, organizations can significantly reduce the attack surface associated with SSH, ensuring that this critical remote access protocol remains a trusted and resilient component of their security infrastructure. SSH hardening strengthens the confidentiality, integrity, and availability of systems while supporting compliance with security frameworks and regulatory requirements in both traditional and cloud-native environments.

SSH for Secure Database Access

Databases are among the most sensitive assets in any IT infrastructure, often containing critical business data, personally identifiable information, or proprietary intellectual property. For this reason, securing database access is a top priority for system administrators and security professionals. SSH is a widely adopted solution to enhance the security of database access by providing a secure, encrypted channel for client-server communication. By tunneling database connections through SSH, organizations can protect sensitive data from interception and eavesdropping, particularly when accessing databases across untrusted networks.

Many traditional database management systems, such as MySQL, PostgreSQL, MongoDB, and Oracle, offer native client-server communication without encryption. When these databases are accessed over public or internal networks without additional security measures, the data transmitted—including queries, results, and potentially user credentials—can be vulnerable to interception by attackers with network access. SSH mitigates this risk by encapsulating the database traffic within an encrypted tunnel, ensuring that the data is shielded from unauthorized observation and tampering.

A common method of securing database connections with SSH is local port forwarding. This involves creating a secure tunnel between the client machine and the remote server hosting the database. The SSH client binds a local port on the client device and forwards all traffic sent to that port through the SSH tunnel to the remote server's database port. For example, an administrator working from a local machine can use SSH to securely forward traffic to a remote PostgreSQL server by running a command such as ssh -L 5432:localhost:5432 user@remote-server. The database client on the local machine then connects to localhost:5432 as if the database were running locally, while the traffic is securely routed through the SSH tunnel to the actual database on the remote server.

This approach provides several advantages. First, it eliminates the need to expose database ports to the public internet. Database servers often operate on well-known ports, such as 3306 for MySQL or 5432 for PostgreSQL, making them attractive targets for attackers performing automated scans. By using SSH tunneling, the database can be configured to listen on localhost only, preventing direct external connections while still allowing remote administrators or applications to securely access the service through the SSH tunnel.

Second, SSH tunneling supports role-based access control and fine-grained firewall rules. Instead of opening database ports to wide IP ranges, administrators can limit SSH access to trusted IP addresses or VPN endpoints. This reduces the attack surface while still enabling remote access for authorized personnel. Security groups, iptables, or cloud-native firewall rules can be configured to permit inbound SSH traffic while denying direct access to the database port from external networks.

In addition to local port forwarding, SSH also supports remote port forwarding, where a port on the remote server is bound and forwards traffic back to the client. This can be useful when exposing a database running on a local machine to a remote system, such as allowing a cloud-based application to access a development database running on a developer's workstation. SSH dynamic port forwarding, which creates a SOCKS proxy, can also be used to route database traffic through a tunnel when combined with appropriate client configurations or proxy-aware tools.

SSH tunneling is commonly used in development and testing environments where engineers require secure access to staging or production databases from remote locations. By using SSH, developers can query or manage databases without needing to connect to corporate VPNs or reconfigure database firewalls. This increases agility while maintaining strong encryption and access control.

In automated workflows, such as CI/CD pipelines or backup scripts, SSH provides a secure method for interacting with databases during deployment or maintenance tasks. Automated jobs can establish SSH tunnels as part of the pipeline execution to perform tasks like running database migrations, exporting data, or synchronizing schema changes. These tunnels can be created on-demand and torn down once the task is complete, limiting the window of exposure.

To enhance security further, SSH tunneling can be combined with SSH key-based authentication and multi-factor authentication (MFA). By disabling password-based SSH logins and requiring key pairs, organizations reduce the risk of brute force attacks and credential theft. Incorporating MFA for SSH access ensures that only verified users with a second authentication factor can establish the necessary tunnels.

While SSH tunneling provides strong encryption and access control, it is not without operational considerations. Idle tunnels can consume system resources or create lingering connections that may conflict with other sessions. Administrators should implement timeout settings, such as ClientAliveInterval, to automatically close inactive SSH sessions. In environments with many users, session monitoring and logging help ensure that tunnels are used appropriately and are not exploited to bypass security controls.

Organizations must also ensure that SSH tunnels do not inadvertently violate network segmentation or compliance policies. For example, in highly segmented environments, tunnels may bridge restricted zones if not properly controlled. To prevent this, SSH tunneling permissions can be limited through server configurations using directives like PermitOpen and AllowTcpForwarding. These settings restrict which ports and destinations can be forwarded through SSH tunnels, reducing the likelihood of misuse.

For teams managing multiple databases across distributed environments, automating SSH tunnel creation is essential. Tools such as autossh can automatically re-establish tunnels if they are dropped, ensuring reliable access during critical operations. Infrastructure-as-code frameworks like Terraform or Ansible can incorporate SSH tunneling as part of the provisioning process, automatically configuring secure connections between application servers and remote databases.

SSH also integrates well with bastion hosts, which act as intermediaries for secure access to internal systems. By tunneling database connections through a bastion host, organizations can enforce centralized access policies, monitor traffic, and log all database access attempts through a controlled entry point. Bastion hosts can be combined with session recording tools to capture full audit trails of administrative sessions interacting with databases, supporting compliance requirements and forensic investigations.

SSH's flexibility and reliability make it a trusted method for securing database access across a wide variety of use cases. Whether used by administrators for direct database management, developers for testing and development, or automated systems for data processing tasks, SSH ensures that sensitive data remains protected from end to end. By tunneling database traffic through encrypted connections and leveraging SSH's authentication and access control features, organizations can enhance the security and integrity of their critical data assets in both on-premises and cloud-native environments.

SSH in Hybrid and Multi-Cloud Deployments

SSH plays a vital role in hybrid and multi-cloud deployments, serving as the primary mechanism for secure remote access, infrastructure management, and interconnectivity between disparate environments. As enterprises increasingly adopt hybrid models—combining on-premises infrastructure with public cloud resources—or leverage multiple cloud providers to avoid vendor lock-in, the need for a secure, standardized method of managing diverse systems becomes paramount. SSH offers a universal, trusted solution that seamlessly bridges the operational gaps across clouds, regions, and private data centers.

In hybrid cloud scenarios, organizations operate workloads both in their own data centers and in public cloud platforms such as AWS, Azure, or Google Cloud. These environments may host critical services, virtual machines, container clusters, and databases that require secure and consistent administrative access. SSH enables system administrators, developers, and automation tools to manage infrastructure across these environments without compromising security. Whether accessing bare-metal servers in a private rack or virtual machines in a cloud provider's infrastructure, SSH provides an encrypted tunnel that protects credentials, commands, and data in transit.

Multi-cloud environments introduce additional complexity by involving two or more public cloud providers. Each provider may have its own networking architecture, identity management systems, and firewall configurations. SSH acts as a neutral protocol that transcends vendor-specific solutions, allowing teams to maintain operational consistency when managing instances, containers, and services across clouds. In practice, this means that an administrator can use SSH to securely access a Linux server on AWS, then pivot to a node running in Azure or GCP using the same SSH tooling and practices.

A major use case of SSH in hybrid and multi-cloud environments is facilitating secure network bridging between clouds and on-premises data centers. In traditional setups, organizations rely on VPNs, direct interconnects, or cloud peering services to link environments. SSH complements these solutions by providing secure tunnels for specific services or tasks. For example, SSH port forwarding can be used to securely access a private database hosted in an on-premises network from an application server running in a public cloud. By tunneling traffic through an SSH session, administrators avoid exposing sensitive services to the public internet while maintaining secure and controlled communication channels.

In hybrid deployments, bastion hosts, also known as jump boxes, are commonly implemented to manage access to internal systems located within private networks or VPCs. Bastion hosts serve as hardened gateways that enforce centralized access controls, logging, and auditing. SSH is the primary protocol used to connect to these bastion hosts. Once inside, administrators can initiate additional SSH sessions to internal systems across hybrid or multi-cloud infrastructures. Organizations often deploy bastion hosts in each environment—on-premises and in each cloud region—to ensure secure entry points wherever infrastructure resides.

Automation plays a critical role in hybrid and multi-cloud operations. Infrastructure-as-Code (IaC) tools such as Terraform, Ansible, and Pulumi leverage SSH to automate provisioning, configuration, and maintenance of resources across multiple environments. For example, an Ansible playbook may use SSH to configure web servers in AWS while simultaneously managing a database cluster running in a private data center. This consistent approach allows DevOps teams to apply the same security policies, configurations, and deployment pipelines regardless of the underlying cloud provider.

Continuous integration and deployment pipelines also rely heavily on SSH to move artifacts and execute remote commands across hybrid and multi-cloud systems. During deployment workflows, CI/CD tools such as Jenkins or GitLab CI/CD use SSH to securely connect to application servers, deploy code, and manage services across different cloud regions or private infrastructure. By leveraging SSH, these workflows ensure that sensitive credentials and deployment payloads are transmitted securely, even when spanning different providers or geographic locations.

One of the challenges in hybrid and multi-cloud environments is managing SSH keys at scale. With infrastructure spread across different platforms, manual key management quickly becomes unsustainable. Organizations often adopt centralized SSH key management systems or SSH certificate authorities to automate the generation, distribution, and rotation of keys or certificates. These systems integrate with identity providers or privileged access management (PAM) platforms to enforce strong authentication and authorization policies consistently across all environments.

Security is a critical consideration when using SSH in hybrid and multi-cloud setups. Exposing SSH ports directly to the internet can make servers vulnerable to brute-force attacks and other threats. To mitigate this risk, many organizations implement strict firewall rules, security groups, and private IP-only access for SSH traffic, ensuring that connections are only permitted from trusted networks, such as corporate VPNs or bastion hosts. Additionally, advanced SSH configurations such as disabling password authentication, restricting agent forwarding, and limiting port forwarding are applied uniformly across all environments to reduce attack surfaces.

SSH also supports secure inter-process communication between services operating in different clouds. For instance, microservices running in Kubernetes clusters on separate cloud providers may require secure communication for database access, message queues, or monitoring agents. SSH tunnels can facilitate these connections, particularly when services must interact across different VPCs or regions with limited peering options. By encapsulating service traffic within SSH tunnels, organizations add an extra layer of encryption and access control beyond standard application-layer security.

SSH monitoring and auditing are equally essential in these complex environments. Security teams must ensure that all SSH activity is logged and centralized, providing visibility into who is accessing systems, from where, and what actions are being performed. This is especially important in multi-cloud architectures where logs can easily become fragmented across different provider ecosystems. Integrating

SSH logs into a unified Security Information and Event Management (SIEM) platform allows teams to detect anomalies, such as unauthorized access attempts or suspicious tunneling activity, across all clouds and data centers.

As hybrid and multi-cloud adoption grows, many organizations are shifting toward zero trust principles, where every access request, including SSH sessions, must be continuously verified and monitored. In this model, SSH is integrated with dynamic access controls, time-limited credentials, and multi-factor authentication to ensure that only verified users and systems can initiate connections across the hybrid environment.

The versatility of SSH ensures that it will continue to play a foundational role in managing and securing hybrid and multi-cloud deployments. Its ability to provide secure, encrypted access across vastly different infrastructures, automate administrative workflows, and support secure data flows between systems makes SSH indispensable to modern IT operations. As environments become more distributed and heterogeneous, SSH remains a reliable and flexible tool to bridge gaps, enhance security, and unify management across on-premises, private cloud, and multi-cloud ecosystems.

SSH and Container Orchestration

As containerized applications and microservices architectures have become dominant in modern IT environments, container orchestration platforms like Kubernetes, Docker Swarm, and OpenShift have emerged as the standard for managing container lifecycles. While container orchestration abstracts much of the infrastructure management from end users, SSH remains a critical tool for administrators and DevOps teams who need to manage, troubleshoot, and maintain the underlying systems running these orchestration platforms. SSH provides secure, low-level access to the nodes that make up container clusters, supporting tasks that are often beyond the scope of automated orchestration tools.

In Kubernetes, for example, the control plane manages the scheduling, scaling, and deployment of containers across worker nodes. These nodes are typically virtual machines or physical servers operating behind the scenes to run container workloads. Although Kubernetes provides API-driven interfaces and tools like kubectl to manage applications, situations regularly arise where administrators must SSH directly into nodes. This might be necessary to perform system-level diagnostics, patch the operating system, debug networking issues, or analyze container runtime problems that are not exposed through Kubernetes APIs.

SSH is particularly useful when troubleshooting node-level problems. If a Kubernetes node becomes unresponsive or if pods consistently fail on a particular worker node, administrators often initiate an SSH session to investigate resource utilization, check system logs, and analyze networking configurations. SSH provides direct access to tools like journalctl, systemctl, netstat, and tcpdump, allowing teams to diagnose issues at the OS and kernel level, which may be contributing to orchestration failures.

Container orchestration platforms rely on a distributed system of components that must work together seamlessly. Kubernetes, for instance, depends on kubelet agents, container runtimes such as containerd or CRI-O, and networking plugins like Calico or Flannel. When troubleshooting problems related to pod scheduling, storage mounts, or inter-pod communication, SSH access to the nodes allows operators to inspect the logs and runtime configurations of these components in detail. While kubectl provides a high-level abstraction for interacting with the cluster, SSH complements it by granting full visibility into the host system.

Beyond diagnostics, SSH plays an important role in the configuration and automation of container orchestration platforms. Infrastructure-as-Code tools such as Terraform, Ansible, and Chef frequently use SSH as their transport mechanism to bootstrap nodes during the initial provisioning of clusters. SSH is leveraged to install Kubernetes components, configure system parameters like sysctl settings, set up container runtimes, and apply security hardening. Even in managed Kubernetes services like Amazon EKS, Google GKE, or Azure AKS, custom workloads or infrastructure enhancements may require direct node access, for which SSH is indispensable.

In hybrid and multi-cloud environments where container orchestration platforms span on-premises data centers and public cloud regions, SSH helps unify administrative workflows. Teams can use SSH to consistently manage nodes across different providers, applying system updates, deploying monitoring agents, and configuring networking rules. SSH tunneling is also used to create secure connections between isolated Kubernetes clusters in separate environments, enabling secure data exchange between microservices operating across different domains.

Security is a crucial aspect when using SSH within container orchestration environments. Given that nodes often run multiple workloads from different teams or projects, enforcing strict access controls and audit mechanisms is essential. SSH access to nodes should be tightly restricted to trusted administrators, and public keys should be managed centrally with frequent rotations to minimize the risk of unauthorized access. Organizations frequently configure SSH servers on nodes to disable password authentication and limit access to specific IP ranges, reducing the attack surface in cloud-native environments.

To further enhance security and streamline workflows, some organizations integrate SSH access with Kubernetes Role-Based Access Control (RBAC) policies and identity providers. For example, SSH certificates or ephemeral SSH keys may be issued dynamically based on the user's Kubernetes role or identity, ensuring that only authorized personnel with the appropriate permissions can access specific nodes within the cluster. This tight integration between cluster-level access controls and node-level SSH permissions supports the principle of least privilege and improves security posture.

While SSH is traditionally associated with server management, it can also be used to interact with containers directly. Administrators may SSH into a node and use tools like docker exec or crictl to enter running containers for troubleshooting purposes. Although Kubernetes provides the kubectl exec command for similar functionality, direct access via SSH and container runtimes may be necessary when kubelet or API server components are malfunctioning or when working with non-Kubernetes container platforms such as Docker Swarm.

SSH is also important for managing and securing the networking layers that support container orchestration. Service meshes, ingress controllers, and overlay networks require proper configuration and monitoring to ensure reliable communication between microservices. When connectivity problems arise, administrators often SSH into nodes to inspect iptables rules, verify route tables, or capture traffic using packet analysis tools. This hands-on access to the underlying networking stack is crucial in diagnosing and resolving complex issues that can impact the availability and performance of containerized applications.

Automated cluster scaling operations also benefit from SSH. Many organizations configure autoscaling groups that add or remove nodes from their clusters based on workload demands. SSH is used by configuration management tools to bootstrap these new nodes, ensuring they are properly configured and integrated into the orchestration platform before workloads are scheduled on them. Automation scripts leverage SSH to apply necessary system updates, configure security policies, and install monitoring agents to maintain consistency and observability across the cluster.

Monitoring and auditing SSH sessions within container orchestration environments is another important consideration. Centralized logging solutions collect SSH session logs from all nodes, ensuring that security teams can detect unauthorized access attempts or policy violations. Session recording tools may also be used in regulated industries to capture full command histories and terminal outputs for compliance and forensic purposes.

As container orchestration platforms continue to evolve, SSH remains a critical enabler of operational excellence. It provides direct, secure access to the foundational layer upon which containerized workloads run. Whether used for node provisioning, debugging, automation, or system-level maintenance, SSH is an essential part of any team's toolkit when managing distributed container environments at scale. Its combination of versatility, security, and reliability ensures that SSH will continue to play a vital role in the success of modern cloud-native infrastructures.

Using SSH with Ansible and Automation Tools

SSH is a cornerstone of modern IT automation, and its integration with tools like Ansible has revolutionized how organizations manage infrastructure. Ansible, a powerful open-source automation platform, leverages SSH as its default communication protocol to securely connect to remote systems, execute tasks, and enforce configurations without requiring any additional agent software. This agentless model makes Ansible highly adaptable across different environments, from on-premises servers to cloud instances and edge devices. SSH provides the secure transport layer that enables Ansible to interact with these systems reliably and efficiently.

At the core of Ansible's design is the ability to automate repetitive administrative tasks such as software installation, user management, system updates, and configuration enforcement. Using SSH as its transport, Ansible connects to remote systems defined in its inventory file and runs modules that perform specific actions. These modules could include copying files, managing services, configuring network settings, or applying security hardening. Since Ansible relies on SSH, there is no need to deploy additional agents or daemons on the target hosts, which reduces operational overhead and simplifies integration with existing infrastructure.

The flexibility of SSH enhances Ansible's scalability. Ansible playbooks can manage hundreds or thousands of remote systems simultaneously, executing tasks over parallel SSH sessions. This is achieved by using asynchronous connections and configurable parallelism, which allows administrators to control how many SSH sessions are active at a given time. The SSH connections are initiated from a control node, typically a workstation or dedicated automation server, and Ansible uses these connections to remotely execute commands and transfer files securely.

Key-based authentication is the preferred method for integrating SSH with Ansible workflows. By configuring SSH key pairs, Ansible can establish passwordless, secure connections to remote systems, enabling fully automated runs without manual intervention. SSH private keys are stored securely on the control node and used by Ansible to authenticate to target hosts. For environments where security requirements are high, SSH keys can be protected with strong passphrases and supplemented with additional mechanisms such as SSH certificates or integration with secrets management platforms like HashiCorp Vault.

SSH is also instrumental when Ansible is used in dynamic environments, such as cloud-native or hybrid infrastructures. Cloud providers like AWS, Azure, and Google Cloud often rely on SSH for administrative access to virtual machines. Ansible can dynamically query these environments using dynamic inventory scripts or plugins, retrieve details about active instances, and initiate SSH connections to manage them in real-time. This capability allows teams to automate provisioning, configuration, and scaling operations in rapidly changing infrastructures.

The use of SSH within Ansible extends beyond configuration management into continuous deployment and orchestration. CI/CD pipelines frequently integrate Ansible tasks to deploy applications, update configurations, and restart services on remote servers. SSH ensures that these operations are performed over secure, encrypted channels. For example, when a pipeline triggers a deployment job, Ansible can use SSH to connect to web servers, upload application artifacts, configure web servers, and manage service lifecycles, all as part of an automated workflow.

Beyond Ansible, other automation tools like Fabric, Capistrano, and SaltStack also leverage SSH as a core transport mechanism. Fabric, a Python-based automation tool, uses SSH to execute commands on remote systems and automate deployment workflows. It provides developers with a simple interface to perform tasks such as running remote shell commands, uploading files, and rebooting servers, all secured by SSH. Capistrano, commonly used for application deployment, utilizes SSH to automate the process of pushing code to remote servers and managing application release lifecycles.

SaltStack, although often deployed with a master-minion architecture, also supports SSH-based execution through its salt-ssh module. This enables administrators to manage systems where installing a minion agent is impractical, allowing SaltStack to operate in a fully agentless mode similar to Ansible. By using SSH as a secure transport layer, SaltStack can remotely execute state files, apply configurations, and run ad hoc commands across managed nodes.

Automation scripts written in languages such as Bash, Python, or Ruby frequently incorporate SSH commands or SSH-based libraries like Paramiko. These scripts automate administrative tasks ranging from patch management to backup orchestration. For instance, a Python script using Paramiko can securely connect to a group of servers, retrieve log files, and synchronize them to a central storage system via SSH tunnels or SFTP. This approach streamlines manual workflows and ensures that sensitive data is transmitted securely between systems.

SSH also plays a key role in enabling hybrid workflows that combine infrastructure-as-code (IaC) tools with configuration management platforms. For example, Terraform may be used to provision cloud infrastructure such as virtual machines, load balancers, and networking resources, while Ansible follows up by using SSH to configure those newly provisioned instances. This separation of responsibilities enables teams to maintain clear boundaries between provisioning and configuration, while SSH provides the secure communication channel for Ansible to execute its tasks across the freshly created infrastructure.

In secure environments, SSH access can be further enhanced by combining automation tools with bastion hosts. Ansible and other tools can be configured to connect to remote systems via SSH jump hosts, enforcing additional layers of security. By funneling SSH traffic through bastion hosts, organizations centralize access control and audit SSH connections, while automation tools retain the ability to manage internal systems located within isolated private networks or virtual private clouds (VPCs).

The ability to use SSH with automation tools also supports compliance and governance initiatives. SSH logs can be collected and analyzed to ensure that automated tasks follow approved policies and procedures. When combined with centralized logging solutions or SIEM platforms, organizations gain full visibility into the actions performed by automation tools over SSH, including changes to system configurations, user accounts, and application deployments. This traceability is critical for regulated industries that require detailed records of administrative activities.

SSH's seamless integration with Ansible and other automation platforms underpins the modern DevOps philosophy of automating everything. From provisioning and configuration management to application deployment and disaster recovery workflows, SSH enables secure and efficient automation across complex IT environments. As organizations continue to embrace automation to increase agility, reduce operational overhead, and improve system consistency, the role of SSH as the trusted transport layer remains a fundamental part of these workflows. Its simplicity, portability, and robust security make SSH an indispensable component of the automation ecosystem, empowering teams to manage infrastructure with confidence and control.

Protecting SSH from Man-in-the-Middle Attacks

SSH is renowned for providing encrypted, secure communication between clients and servers. However, like all network protocols, it is not immune to the risk of man-in-the-middle (MITM) attacks. In an MITM attack, a malicious actor intercepts or alters communication between two parties without their knowledge, potentially capturing sensitive information or injecting malicious commands. Although SSH employs strong encryption to safeguard data in transit, if the initial trust establishment process is compromised, an attacker can still insert themselves into the communication stream. Protecting SSH from MITM attacks requires a layered approach that includes verifying host identities, enforcing strict policies, and following secure operational practices.

At the heart of SSH's protection against MITM attacks is its use of host key verification. When an SSH client connects to a server for the first time, the server presents its public host key. The client can either verify this key against a known value or, by default, store it in the user's known_hosts file. Subsequent connections to the same server will compare the presented key to the stored value. If the key does not match, SSH will issue a warning, signaling that the connection may have been intercepted or the server reinstalled or replaced. However, many users bypass this warning out of convenience, accepting the new key without verifying its authenticity, creating an opportunity for an MITM attack to succeed.

One of the most important defenses against MITM attacks in SSH is enforcing strict host key verification policies. Administrators should never disable host key checking or automatically accept new host keys in scripts without verification. Instead, known_hosts files should be populated with verified public host keys before users or automation tools connect to the servers. This can be accomplished manually by administrators or through automated configuration management tools like Ansible, which can distribute known host keys across managed systems. Ensuring that all connections are made only to servers with trusted, pre-verified host keys eliminates a common entry point for attackers attempting to impersonate a server.

Another effective method for preventing MITM attacks is the use of SSH certificates issued by a trusted certificate authority (CA). SSH certificates operate similarly to SSL/TLS certificates in that they allow servers to prove their identity based on a trusted CA signature, rather than a static key. By deploying a centralized SSH CA and configuring clients to trust the CA's public key, administrators can remove the reliance on individual known_hosts files and reduce the risk of accepting rogue host keys. SSH certificates provide a scalable and secure approach to host verification, especially in dynamic or large-scale environments where servers are frequently added or removed.

DNS spoofing is another technique commonly associated with MITM attacks on SSH sessions. If an attacker can manipulate DNS responses, they may redirect a client to an attacker-controlled server, which then attempts to impersonate the legitimate server. To mitigate this, organizations should use DNS security extensions (DNSSEC) to protect against DNS spoofing and ensure the integrity of DNS responses. Additionally, relying on static IP addresses or securely configured internal DNS servers can reduce the likelihood of DNS-based redirection.

Strict firewall policies and network segmentation also help reduce the risk of MITM attacks by limiting the exposure of SSH services to trusted networks only. By ensuring that SSH servers are not accessible from untrusted or public networks unless necessary, organizations make it more difficult for attackers to position themselves between clients and servers. In scenarios where remote access is required from external networks, enforcing access through a secure bastion host or VPN ensures that communication occurs over controlled and monitored paths.

To further strengthen protection against MITM attacks, administrators should implement multi-factor authentication (MFA) for SSH access. While MFA does not prevent MITM on its own, it provides an additional barrier that requires attackers to possess a second factor, such as a hardware token or mobile authenticator, to successfully compromise an SSH session. This significantly reduces the likelihood of a successful attack, even if the attacker manages to intercept login credentials during the connection process.

SSH also supports additional configuration settings to help detect and prevent MITM attempts. For example, the VisualHostKey option, when enabled in the SSH client configuration, displays a graphical hash fingerprint of the server's host key during the connection process. This provides a visual cue that allows users to verify the server's identity against known fingerprints. While not foolproof, this additional information can help attentive users spot discrepancies that may indicate a MITM attempt.

Enforcing strict cryptographic policies is equally important. Administrators should configure SSH servers and clients to only use modern, secure algorithms for key exchange, encryption, and message authentication. By disabling outdated algorithms such as diffie-hellman-group1-sha1 or 3des-cbc, organizations reduce the likelihood of downgrade attacks, where an attacker forces the connection to use weaker cryptography that could be more easily broken or manipulated.

Network-level protections such as encrypted VPN tunnels further complement SSH's native encryption. When SSH traffic is encapsulated within a VPN tunnel, attackers would need to compromise both the VPN and SSH layers to successfully carry out a MITM attack. This layered approach to encryption adds redundancy and increases the complexity for potential attackers.

Logging and monitoring are critical components of detecting and responding to MITM attempts. SSH servers should be configured to log all connection attempts, including key mismatches and authentication failures. Anomalies such as repeated attempts from unexpected IP addresses, sudden key changes, or connections from geographically unusual locations may indicate an ongoing MITM campaign or other forms of attack. These logs should be forwarded to a centralized SIEM platform, where they can be correlated with other security events to enable rapid detection and response.

User training is an often-overlooked yet essential component in preventing MITM attacks. Many successful MITM attacks rely on social engineering or user inattention, such as ignoring host key mismatch warnings. By educating users about the risks of MITM, the importance of host key verification, and secure SSH usage practices, organizations strengthen their defenses. Users should be encouraged to report suspicious activity, such as unexpected prompts or key changes, to security teams for investigation.

While SSH is inherently secure by design, protecting it from MITM attacks requires a multi-layered strategy. Combining strict host key management, the use of SSH certificates, modern cryptographic configurations, network segmentation, and vigilant monitoring creates a robust defensive posture. By taking these measures, organizations can confidently rely on SSH as a secure means of remote access, even in environments where adversaries may attempt to intercept or manipulate communications.

Two-Factor Authentication for SSH

As organizations face an ever-growing landscape of cyber threats, relying on a single layer of protection such as traditional username and password combinations for SSH access is no longer sufficient. Two-factor authentication, commonly referred to as 2FA, has emerged as one of the most effective methods to strengthen security by requiring an additional verification step beyond the standard login credentials. When applied to SSH, 2FA adds an extra barrier that prevents unauthorized access, even if an attacker manages to compromise a user's password or private key.

Two-factor authentication operates on the principle of combining two independent categories of credentials: something you know, such as a password or private key, and something you have, such as a hardware token, mobile device, or one-time password generator. By enforcing both factors during the SSH login process, organizations significantly reduce the likelihood of unauthorized access, as attackers would need to gain control over both factors simultaneously.

One of the most widely used methods of implementing 2FA for SSH is through time-based one-time password (TOTP) systems. This approach integrates applications such as Google Authenticator, Authy, or FreeOTP with the SSH authentication workflow. When a user initiates an SSH connection, they are prompted to enter not only their password or use their SSH key but also a TOTP generated on their personal device. The TOTP is typically valid for only 30 seconds, making it virtually impossible for attackers to reuse a captured code. The implementation involves installing a PAM (Pluggable Authentication Module) on the server, such as libpam-google-authenticator, and configuring the SSH server to enforce the additional step before granting access.

For high-security environments, hardware-based tokens such as YubiKeys provide an even stronger layer of protection. YubiKeys can be configured to generate TOTP codes or operate in challenge-response modes where the SSH server sends a cryptographic challenge to the token, which then generates a secure response that authenticates the user. These hardware tokens offer resistance to phishing and malware attacks since the secrets used to generate responses are never exposed to the host system or network. Some organizations also integrate smart cards or PIV (Personal Identity Verification) cards with SSH, leveraging existing corporate ID cards or government-issued credentials as the second factor.

Another popular method for implementing 2FA for SSH is via push-based authentication. This system relies on a mobile app to send push notifications when a user attempts to log in via SSH. Upon receiving the push notification, the user must approve or deny the login attempt directly from their device. Duo Security, a widely adopted 2FA solution, offers such functionality and provides extensive integration options for SSH, along with additional features like device health checks and policy enforcement.

In corporate settings where centralized identity and access management is essential, organizations often integrate SSH 2FA with existing identity providers. This includes leveraging services like LDAP, Active Directory, or SSO platforms in combination with multi-factor authentication policies enforced at the directory level. By using federated authentication, organizations ensure that all remote access attempts via SSH conform to broader corporate security policies, including password complexity, user deprovisioning, and multi-factor enforcement across other applications.

To configure SSH servers for two-factor authentication, administrators typically modify the sshd_config file to enable ChallengeResponseAuthentication and ensure that PAM is used for authentication control. The PAM configuration is then updated to include the appropriate module, such as pam_google_authenticator.so or pam_duo.so, which triggers the 2FA challenge. Once configured, SSH sessions will prompt for both the primary credential and the secondary factor before granting shell access.

While two-factor authentication adds a critical layer of protection, it must be implemented thoughtfully to avoid negatively impacting operational workflows. For instance, automated scripts, monitoring tools, and CI/CD pipelines that rely on SSH key-based access should be exempt from 2FA challenges or use alternative secure methods such as short-lived SSH certificates issued via an automated approval process. It is common to create separate roles or accounts for automation tasks, with strict key management and limited privileges, while reserving 2FA-enforced accounts for human administrators.

Emergency access scenarios also require careful planning when implementing 2FA for SSH. If a user loses their mobile device or hardware token, secure backup mechanisms should be available to allow access without compromising security. This might include enrolling multiple devices, generating recovery codes during the initial 2FA setup, or having a documented break-glass procedure that involves higher-level approval for account recovery.

Monitoring and logging play an important role in maintaining visibility into 2FA-enabled SSH systems. All 2FA challenges, successes, and failures should be logged and sent to centralized logging or SIEM systems. Anomalies such as repeated failed 2FA attempts, login attempts from unusual geographic locations, or attempts to bypass 2FA through unauthorized configuration changes should trigger alerts and be subject to incident response procedures.

User training and awareness are equally important. While 2FA significantly increases security, its effectiveness relies on users understanding its importance and following best practices. Users should be trained to recognize phishing attempts, avoid approving suspicious push notifications, and report lost or stolen authentication devices immediately.

SSH two-factor authentication also aligns with regulatory and compliance requirements. Standards such as PCI DSS, HIPAA, and NIST guidelines recommend or mandate the use of multi-factor authentication for administrative access to systems handling sensitive data. Implementing 2FA for SSH helps organizations meet these requirements and demonstrate a commitment to protecting critical infrastructure.

While SSH is inherently secure due to its use of cryptographic protocols, the addition of two-factor authentication addresses one of its key vulnerabilities: the human factor. Passwords can be weak, shared, or stolen, and even SSH keys can be lost or inadvertently exposed. By layering a second factor into the authentication process, organizations create a more resilient security model that significantly reduces the risk of unauthorized remote access. Whether using time-based tokens, hardware keys, push notifications, or smart cards, 2FA is a proven and practical enhancement that strengthens the integrity of SSH access in any environment.

SSH and VPN: Complementary Tools

SSH and VPN are two of the most widely used technologies for securing remote access and data communication across untrusted networks. Both serve the purpose of providing encryption and safeguarding sensitive data in transit, but they do so in different ways and operate at different layers of the networking stack. Rather than viewing SSH and VPN as competing solutions, many organizations recognize that these tools complement each other, each bringing unique strengths to network security and remote access strategies.

SSH, or Secure Shell, operates at the application layer and is primarily used to establish encrypted connections between a client and a server for the purpose of remote command execution, file transfers, and port forwarding. SSH is commonly favored by system administrators, developers, and automation tools for securely managing servers, executing scripts, and transferring files over insecure networks. SSH sessions are established on-demand, with the client initiating a direct connection to the server, typically over port 22. SSH excels in scenarios where secure access to a specific server or set of servers is required without the overhead of a full network-level tunnel.

VPN, or Virtual Private Network, on the other hand, functions at the network layer, creating an encrypted tunnel between a client and a remote network. VPNs are used to securely bridge entire networks or allow clients to appear as though they are part of a remote private network. VPN technologies such as OpenVPN, WireGuard, and IPsec enable users to securely access all resources within a remote network, including servers, databases, internal websites, and other services, as if they were directly connected to the private LAN. VPNs are particularly effective for organizations that require secure access to a broad range of internal systems and services for remote employees or distributed teams.

The complementary nature of SSH and VPN becomes clear when considering use cases that require both granular access to specific hosts and broader access to internal resources. For example, an administrator working remotely may first connect to a corporate VPN, which provides encrypted access to the internal network and allows the administrator to reach internal IP addresses not exposed to the public internet. Once on the VPN, the administrator can then initiate SSH sessions to specific servers within the internal network to perform tasks such as system updates, configuration management, or log reviews.

In this scenario, the VPN serves as the first layer of defense, creating a secure perimeter around the corporate network and limiting access to trusted users and devices. SSH provides the second layer, securing individual sessions and operations on specific hosts. By combining VPN and SSH, organizations can enforce security at both the network and application levels, reducing the risk of unauthorized access and improving the overall security posture.

SSH also complements VPNs in environments where network segmentation and access control are critical. While VPNs typically provide access to a wide range of network resources, SSH can be used to enforce more granular access policies. For example, even after connecting to a VPN, users may only be permitted to SSH into specific servers or subnets based on their roles and responsibilities. This approach aligns with the principle of least privilege by ensuring that users have access only to the resources necessary to perform their duties.

SSH tunneling, a feature of SSH that allows port forwarding over an encrypted channel, can also be used alongside VPNs to create secure connections to specific services. An administrator connected to a VPN may still choose to tunnel sensitive application traffic over SSH to add an additional layer of encryption and access control. For instance, a developer might SSH into a bastion host over the VPN and forward traffic to a database server, thereby creating a secure path that limits direct access to the database while logging all SSH activity for auditing purposes.

Another common scenario involves using SSH as a fallback or lightweight alternative to VPNs. While VPNs are effective for persistent network-level access, they can introduce latency, require additional software or client configuration, and depend on centralized VPN servers that may become single points of failure. SSH, by contrast, is lightweight, widely supported, and can be quickly deployed in ad-hoc situations where setting up a VPN is impractical. For example, when troubleshooting an isolated system or managing a cloud-hosted instance that is not part of a corporate VPN, SSH provides immediate, secure access without requiring changes to network infrastructure.

In cloud-native environments, the use of SSH and VPN is further adapted to support hybrid architectures. Many organizations use VPN tunnels to securely connect on-premises data centers to cloud environments, facilitating hybrid cloud models where workloads are distributed across private and public infrastructure. SSH is then used within these connected networks to manage cloud-based virtual machines, containers, or Kubernetes clusters securely. Bastion hosts located within cloud VPCs often act as SSH entry points, accessible only via VPN, further segmenting access and reducing the exposure of critical systems.

Security best practices recommend that VPN and SSH configurations be tightly controlled and audited. For VPNs, this includes implementing multi-factor authentication (MFA), restricting access to specific IP ranges or user groups, and monitoring VPN connections for anomalies. For SSH, this involves disabling password authentication in favor of key-based authentication, rotating SSH keys regularly, restricting SSH access to specific users and IPs, and enforcing session logging and monitoring. Combining these controls ensures that both technologies provide maximum protection when used together.

Additionally, VPN and SSH usage should be incorporated into broader incident response and disaster recovery plans. In the event of a security breach or system compromise, SSH can be used over the VPN tunnel to isolate affected systems, apply patches, and recover services. The ability to remotely and securely manage infrastructure using SSH within a VPN-protected environment enhances an organization's resilience and operational continuity.

SSH and VPN also share synergies in automation and DevOps workflows. Infrastructure-as-code tools like Terraform may be used to automate the deployment of VPN gateways and associated network configurations, while configuration management tools like Ansible leverage SSH to manage individual servers and services within the VPN-protected environment.

SSH and Public Key Infrastructure (PKI)

SSH and Public Key Infrastructure (PKI) are two foundational technologies in modern cybersecurity, each serving distinct yet complementary roles in ensuring the security of digital communication and authentication. SSH is a protocol that allows secure remote access, encrypted file transfers, and command execution over untrusted networks. PKI, on the other hand, is a framework of technologies, policies, and procedures used to create, distribute, manage, and revoke digital certificates that authenticate the identity of users, devices, or services. When integrated together, SSH and PKI significantly enhance identity verification, simplify key management at scale, and increase the trustworthiness of remote connections across organizations.

Traditional SSH key-based authentication relies on generating asymmetric key pairs consisting of a private key and a corresponding public key. The private key remains on the client machine and is used to authenticate the user, while the public key is distributed to the target servers and placed in the authorized_keys file. Although this method is secure and widely adopted, it introduces key management challenges in large environments. Manually distributing, rotating, and revoking public keys across hundreds or thousands of servers can become burdensome and error-prone.

PKI solves this problem by introducing a centralized trust model through Certificate Authorities (CAs). In a PKI system, the CA acts as a trusted third party responsible for issuing and signing digital certificates. These certificates verify the ownership of public keys by binding them to the identities of users or hosts. In the context of SSH, PKI can be leveraged to replace static public keys with short-lived SSH certificates issued by an internal CA. This method streamlines access management, as administrators no longer need to maintain large inventories of static authorized_keys files across multiple servers.

When SSH is integrated with PKI, users authenticate to the internal CA, which validates their identity through mechanisms such as LDAP, SSO, or multi-factor authentication. Upon successful validation, the CA issues a time-limited SSH certificate that includes information about the user's identity, roles, and access permissions. The SSH certificate is then presented to the target server, which has been pre-configured to trust the issuing CA. The server validates the certificate, checks its expiration time, and enforces any associated policies before granting access.

This model introduces several benefits over traditional SSH key management. First, it enables just-in-time (JIT) access, where users only receive access credentials when they need them. Once the certificate expires, the user must request a new one, reducing the risk of credential misuse and ensuring that access is continuously tied to the user's current identity and role. This approach supports the principles of least privilege and zero trust by limiting access based on context and reducing the lifespan of credentials.

PKI also enhances scalability. In environments where infrastructure changes frequently, such as in cloud-native or containerized deployments, SSH certificates can be used to automate secure access to ephemeral instances and dynamically provisioned resources. Rather than updating authorized_keys files every time a new server is spun up or decommissioned, the organization simply configures new servers to trust the CA, greatly simplifying operations.

Host authentication is another critical aspect where SSH and PKI intersect. In traditional SSH workflows, clients rely on storing server public keys in their known_hosts file to detect man-in-the-middle (MITM) attacks. However, managing known_hosts files across large fleets can be as cumbersome as managing authorized_keys files. By using host certificates issued by a CA, administrators can centralize the management of host identities as well. Clients configured to trust the CA will automatically validate the authenticity of any server presenting a host certificate, reducing manual overhead and increasing security.

The integration of PKI with SSH is often implemented using OpenSSH's built-in support for certificate-based authentication. OpenSSH allows administrators to generate a CA key pair, sign user and host keys to produce certificates, and configure SSH servers and clients to validate those certificates against the CA's public key. SSH certificates can include a wide array of metadata, such as principals (usernames or hostnames), valid IP ranges, permitted commands, and expiration times, allowing fine-grained control over access policies.

Automated certificate issuance and renewal are vital for efficient PKI-based SSH environments. Organizations often integrate SSH PKI workflows with automation tools and identity providers. For instance, a developer may authenticate to a certificate authority using a web-based portal protected by SSO and MFA. After successful authentication, a short-lived SSH certificate is generated and automatically installed on the developer's local machine, where it is used for secure access to internal systems. This eliminates the need for manually handling static private-public key pairs while improving auditability and user experience.

In regulated industries or organizations with strict compliance requirements, SSH and PKI integration enhances accountability and supports audit trails. Certificates inherently include user identity information, which can be logged and monitored during SSH sessions. Security teams can track which users accessed which systems, when, and for how long, providing detailed records that assist with compliance reporting and forensic investigations.

The revocation of compromised or outdated credentials is another challenge that PKI addresses effectively. With static SSH keys, removing access typically involves manually editing authorized_keys files on every server where the key was deployed. In contrast, SSH certificates can be revoked centrally by the CA, and servers can be configured to consult Certificate Revocation Lists (CRLs) or Online Certificate Status Protocol (OCSP) responders to reject revoked certificates automatically. This immediate and centralized revocation capability greatly reduces the time window for potential misuse of compromised credentials.

By combining SSH and PKI, organizations achieve a more secure, scalable, and efficient access control model. The centralized trust model provided by PKI simplifies identity management across distributed systems and enables automation of secure access workflows. Whether managing cloud workloads, hybrid infrastructures, or traditional data centers, the integration of SSH with PKI ensures that remote access remains tightly controlled, resilient to attacks, and adaptable to the demands of modern IT environments. The union of these two technologies represents a forward-thinking approach to secure remote management in a world where agility, scalability, and security must coexist.

Centralized SSH Key Management Solutions

Managing SSH keys across a growing infrastructure can quickly become an overwhelming challenge for organizations operating at scale. While SSH provides robust encryption and secure remote access, its traditional key management model is decentralized, where users generate key pairs locally and distribute public keys manually. As environments expand to include hundreds or thousands of servers, cloud instances, and hybrid infrastructure components, the manual handling of SSH keys introduces operational inefficiencies, security risks, and compliance challenges. Centralized SSH key management solutions have emerged to address these issues, providing automated, policy-driven frameworks for managing the lifecycle of SSH keys across distributed systems.

Centralized SSH key management platforms streamline the creation, distribution, rotation, and revocation of SSH keys, all from a single control point. These solutions integrate with directory services, privileged access management systems, and identity providers to ensure that only authorized users can generate and deploy keys in alignment with organizational policies. One of the most significant benefits of centralized key management is the elimination of key sprawl. In unmanaged environments, it is common to encounter orphaned keys left behind by former employees, contractors, or deprecated services. These orphaned keys create backdoors into critical systems and are often overlooked during manual audits. A centralized platform continuously monitors and inventories keys, alerting administrators to unauthorized, expired, or unused keys, reducing the risk of unauthorized access.

Centralized key management platforms also support automated key rotation policies. Rotating SSH keys regularly is a well-established security best practice that reduces the impact of compromised credentials. However, manual rotation processes are resource-intensive and prone to human error. Automated solutions enforce key expiration policies and rotate keys across all managed endpoints without requiring manual intervention. This ensures that keys are consistently replaced in accordance with security policies while minimizing disruption to end-users and automated workflows.

In addition to rotation, centralized platforms enforce uniform access control policies. Administrators can define who is permitted to create or deploy keys, which systems or environments they can access, and under what conditions. These controls are often role-based and tightly integrated with corporate identity systems such as Active Directory or LDAP. By tying SSH key issuance to user identity and role, organizations strengthen their access control models and support least-privilege principles. For example, a developer may be permitted to access only development and staging environments, while production access is restricted to a limited group of senior engineers and subject to additional approval workflows.

Centralized key management also enhances visibility and auditing capabilities. Every key issuance, deployment, rotation, and revocation event is logged and can be forwarded to a centralized Security Information and Event Management (SIEM) system. This provides security teams with a comprehensive view of SSH access activity across the entire organization. Detailed logs support incident response investigations, compliance reporting, and ongoing security assessments. In highly regulated industries, where compliance frameworks such as PCI DSS, HIPAA, or ISO 27001 require strict control and auditability of administrative access, centralized SSH key management helps meet these obligations.

Another key advantage is the ability to automate the provisioning of keys to ephemeral infrastructure. In dynamic environments such as cloud-native applications, Kubernetes clusters, or auto-scaling groups, servers and containers may be created and terminated in rapid succession. Manual key distribution does not scale in these fast-moving environments. Centralized key management solutions integrate with Infrastructure-as-Code tools and cloud provider APIs to automatically provision and deprovision keys as infrastructure changes, ensuring that keys are always in sync with current resource states.

These platforms often extend beyond static keys by supporting SSH certificates, which are short-lived credentials signed by a trusted internal certificate authority (CA). SSH certificates simplify key management further by removing the need to distribute individual public keys to servers. Instead, servers are configured to trust the CA, and users receive signed certificates with defined validity periods and access scopes. Centralized key management platforms automate the process of certificate issuance and expiration, providing a seamless user experience while maintaining high security standards.

Some leading SSH key management solutions also integrate with privileged access management (PAM) systems, combining SSH key control with session monitoring, recording, and approval workflows. This integration creates an additional security layer by requiring users to request access through the PAM system, which then brokers SSH sessions according to organizational policies. PAM integration helps reduce the risk of unauthorized access and enforces real-time monitoring of administrative actions.

In addition to securing human access, centralized platforms manage SSH keys for service accounts and automated processes. Many organizations rely on scripts, CI/CD pipelines, and system services that require SSH-based access to remote servers for deployment, monitoring, or maintenance tasks. Centralized solutions provide secure APIs for programmatically generating temporary keys or certificates for these non-human accounts, reducing the risks associated with hardcoded credentials and improving key lifecycle management.

Cloud-native centralized SSH key management services are also available to organizations that rely on major cloud providers. AWS, for example, offers EC2 Instance Connect, which integrates with IAM to manage SSH access dynamically without requiring persistent keys on instances. Similar services in other cloud platforms allow administrators to control access via native IAM policies, automating access provisioning while maintaining compliance with enterprise security standards.

Adopting centralized SSH key management does require careful planning and a phased implementation approach. Organizations must audit existing keys, identify unused or unauthorized keys, and clean up legacy configurations before transitioning to a centralized system. User training and change management processes are essential to ensure that teams understand the benefits of the new system and adhere to updated workflows. Additionally, integrating centralized key management with existing DevOps pipelines and infrastructure automation tools helps ensure a smooth transition without disrupting productivity.

Centralized SSH key management solutions are essential for modern organizations seeking to scale securely while reducing administrative overhead and mitigating risks. By automating key lifecycle processes, enforcing consistent policies, and providing enhanced visibility into SSH activity, these platforms help organizations address growing security challenges in today's hybrid, multi-cloud, and distributed IT landscapes. Whether managing a small set of critical servers or operating at enterprise scale, centralized SSH key management is a crucial component of a mature and resilient security program.

SSH and Compliance Requirements

SSH is a fundamental tool for secure remote access and administrative control across IT environments, but its usage is closely scrutinized in industries subject to regulatory and compliance requirements. Whether in sectors such as finance, healthcare, government, or e-commerce, organizations are bound by standards that mandate the protection of sensitive data, enforce strict access controls, and require comprehensive auditing of administrative actions. Compliance frameworks like PCI DSS, HIPAA, SOX, GDPR, NIST, and ISO/IEC

27001 all contain elements that impact how SSH is deployed, monitored, and secured within enterprise systems. Ensuring that SSH implementations align with these compliance obligations is a critical aspect of risk management and corporate governance.

One of the most common compliance mandates related to SSH is the enforcement of strong authentication mechanisms. Many regulations require that administrative access to systems handling sensitive data or critical infrastructure must be protected by multi-factor authentication (MFA). While SSH traditionally relies on key-based or password-based authentication, compliance dictates that organizations enhance this by integrating a second factor such as time-based one-time passwords, hardware tokens, or biometric verification. Implementing two-factor authentication with SSH satisfies regulatory requirements and reduces the risk of unauthorized access, addressing concerns outlined in standards like PCI DSS Requirement 8, which focuses on strong access control measures.

Another critical area of compliance is access control and the principle of least privilege. Organizations are required to restrict administrative access strictly to authorized personnel and limit access to only those resources necessary for job functions. SSH configurations must reflect these principles by restricting which users or groups are allowed to establish connections to critical systems. This often involves using directives like AllowUsers or AllowGroups within sshd_config files, configuring firewalls to limit SSH access to trusted IP addresses, and segmenting networks to prevent lateral movement between systems. Compliance frameworks such as NIST SP 800-53 and ISO 27001 emphasize the importance of limiting access based on user roles and responsibilities, which directly impacts how SSH permissions are structured.

Auditability and monitoring are key pillars of virtually all compliance programs. Standards such as HIPAA and SOX require organizations to maintain detailed records of system access and administrative activities. SSH, when properly configured, supports extensive logging capabilities that provide visibility into authentication attempts, successful connections, session start and end times, and other critical events. To meet compliance requirements, organizations must forward SSH logs to centralized logging platforms or Security Information and

Event Management (SIEM) systems, where they can be analyzed, correlated, and stored according to regulatory retention policies. Logs should capture both successful and failed login attempts, as well as the use of sudo or privilege escalation within SSH sessions.

For environments with stringent auditing needs, additional layers such as session recording and command logging may be required. Some compliance regimes mandate the recording of all administrative sessions to enable forensic investigations and demonstrate accountability. This can be accomplished by integrating SSH with privileged access management (PAM) solutions that provide full session recording capabilities. These records, when combined with traditional system logs, offer a comprehensive audit trail of user actions and can be critical in meeting legal and regulatory obligations.

Key management is another area where SSH and compliance intersect. Many organizations face challenges related to managing the lifecycle of SSH keys across large, distributed environments. Compliance frameworks frequently require that cryptographic keys be rotated regularly, access be revoked promptly for terminated employees, and orphaned or unused keys be removed from systems. For example, PCI DSS Requirement 8.3 specifies the importance of secure authentication methods, including managing and revoking authentication credentials. Implementing a centralized SSH key management solution allows organizations to automate key rotation, control key distribution, and reduce the risks associated with key sprawl, while also generating audit logs to demonstrate compliance.

Encryption strength and cryptographic standards are also addressed in many regulations. SSH's native encryption capabilities help meet these requirements, but configurations must be hardened to ensure only modern and secure algorithms are used. Weak or deprecated ciphers such as 3DES or legacy key exchange methods like diffie-hellman-group1-sha1 are discouraged or explicitly prohibited by frameworks such as NIST and PCI DSS. Administrators should review and enforce strict cryptographic policies within the sshd_config file to ensure that only strong algorithms such as aes256-gcm@openssh.com and chacha20-poly1305@openssh.com are enabled, providing a higher level of security and regulatory compliance.

Compliance standards also require organizations to demonstrate that administrative actions are subject to periodic review. This means that SSH access lists, logs, and configurations must be reviewed regularly to ensure they remain aligned with security policies and access control requirements. Access to SSH configuration files, private keys, and sensitive logs should be limited to authorized personnel only, and changes to SSH-related settings must be tracked through change management processes. For example, ISO/IEC 27001 emphasizes the need for regular reviews and audits of access rights and privileged accounts, ensuring that SSH configurations and user entitlements are not left unchecked.

Incident response is another compliance consideration linked to SSH. Organizations must have processes in place to respond quickly to security incidents, such as a compromised SSH key or a suspicious login event. Compliance frameworks typically require that incident response procedures be documented, tested, and updated regularly. SSH logs and session records play a critical role in these processes, providing essential information to identify the source and scope of incidents. By integrating SSH with incident response platforms and automated alerting systems, organizations can meet regulatory expectations for timely and effective incident handling.

Compliance requirements also influence how SSH is used within cloud and hybrid environments. For instance, under GDPR, organizations handling the personal data of EU citizens must ensure that data transfers and access are adequately protected, regardless of where cloud infrastructure is located. When SSH is used to manage virtual machines or cloud-native services, the same compliance principles—strong authentication, secure key management, auditing, and encryption—apply. In hybrid models, SSH often serves as the secure bridge between on-premises and cloud infrastructure, and organizations must ensure that SSH configurations in both environments align with data protection and regulatory mandates.

Finally, compliance with data sovereignty and privacy regulations impacts how SSH is configured to protect data in transit. SSH tunnels used for port forwarding or secure file transfers must ensure that sensitive data is transmitted securely across network boundaries. In some jurisdictions, additional controls may be required to prevent data from being routed through or stored in unauthorized regions. This makes it critical for organizations to document and enforce SSH usage policies that account for data residency and privacy laws applicable to their industry and geographic footprint.

SSH is not just a technical tool; it is a component of an organization's broader security and compliance framework. The secure implementation, monitoring, and management of SSH are essential to meeting regulatory obligations and protecting sensitive assets. By aligning SSH practices with compliance requirements, organizations demonstrate due diligence in safeguarding data and reinforcing trust with customers, partners, and regulatory bodies.

SSH in High-Availability Architectures

High-availability architectures are designed to ensure that systems and services remain operational with minimal downtime, even in the face of hardware failures, network disruptions, or other unforeseen incidents. These architectures often consist of multiple redundant components, including load balancers, clustered servers, and geographically distributed data centers. Within this complex ecosystem, SSH plays a critical role as the foundational mechanism for secure remote management, system monitoring, troubleshooting, and orchestration. The reliability and flexibility of SSH make it indispensable in high-availability environments where uptime and responsiveness are paramount.

SSH provides the secure backbone for administrators and automated systems to manage highly available clusters of servers and services. Whether maintaining web servers behind a load balancer, managing replicated databases, or supporting failover mechanisms across multiple availability zones, SSH enables engineers to execute commands, transfer files, and deploy updates without interrupting critical services. In high-availability setups, it is often necessary to manage large numbers of nodes as a single logical unit, and SSH allows teams to operate efficiently at scale while ensuring encrypted, authenticated communication with every component in the architecture.

One of the key benefits of SSH in high-availability architectures is its ability to support remote management during incident response scenarios. When a node in a cluster fails or a service experiences degraded performance, administrators must be able to quickly access the affected system to investigate and resolve the issue. SSH ensures that even when portions of the infrastructure are under stress, administrators can securely log into nodes, access system logs, restart services, or apply configuration changes. The encrypted nature of SSH protects sensitive operational data during these critical interventions, safeguarding credentials and commands from interception even during network disruptions.

In environments with geographically distributed systems, such as active-active data centers or hybrid cloud deployments, SSH provides a uniform method for securely managing infrastructure across regions. High-availability architectures often include components located in multiple data centers to mitigate the risk of regional outages. With SSH, administrators can maintain consistency across these distributed nodes by remotely configuring services, applying patches, and enforcing security policies from a centralized location. This allows organizations to reduce travel time, minimize operational overhead, and quickly respond to infrastructure needs regardless of where a failure or issue occurs.

Automation is another key pillar of high-availability systems, and SSH is central to these automation workflows. Configuration management tools such as Ansible and SaltStack rely on SSH to connect to each node in a cluster, ensuring that configurations are applied uniformly and without manual intervention. These tools use SSH to deploy services, manage failover scripts, and coordinate updates across redundant systems to maintain consistency while minimizing service disruption. During rolling updates or blue-green deployments, where individual servers are updated incrementally while the remaining infrastructure continues to serve production traffic, SSH enables automated scripts to manage these transitions securely and efficiently.

In high-availability database architectures, SSH provides secure administrative access to clusters running replication or clustering mechanisms such as MySQL Group Replication, PostgreSQL streaming replication, or MongoDB replica sets. When failover events occur, such as a primary node failure triggering a new leader election, administrators often use SSH to verify the health of replication links, inspect lag times, and adjust configurations to restore optimal performance. Secure tunnels established via SSH are also used to remotely access internal management interfaces or database consoles without exposing them to public networks, reducing the attack surface of these mission-critical systems.

Load balancers, which are often the front line of high-availability systems, are typically administered over SSH as well. Administrators use SSH to connect to hardware or software load balancers to update routing configurations, manage SSL/TLS certificates, or troubleshoot traffic anomalies in real time. For example, in the event of a DDoS attack or sudden traffic spike, engineers may SSH into load balancers to adjust rate-limiting rules or distribute traffic across additional backend servers.

SSH is also invaluable for managing virtual machines and containerized environments within high-availability setups. Many organizations deploy clusters of container orchestrators such as Kubernetes or Docker Swarm, and while orchestration platforms provide APIs for day-to-day operations, SSH is often used for deeper system-level interventions. Administrators may SSH into Kubernetes nodes to address underlying operating system issues, inspect logs from container runtimes, or troubleshoot networking configurations affecting service mesh or ingress controllers. In clustered environments where high availability is paramount, the ability to securely access each node individually helps maintain system resilience and operational efficiency.

Security is a major consideration in high-availability environments where SSH is a primary access method. To minimize risk, SSH configurations must be hardened to enforce best practices such as disabling password authentication, using key-based authentication, restricting access by IP address, and limiting root login. In critical systems that require additional layers of protection, multi-factor authentication and centralized identity management are often integrated into SSH workflows. Bastion hosts are frequently deployed as controlled gateways through which all SSH sessions must pass before reaching sensitive systems, providing an additional layer of auditing and access control.

Monitoring and alerting systems in high-availability architectures often rely on SSH to perform health checks and gather telemetry from remote nodes. Tools such as Nagios, Zabbix, and Prometheus may use SSH scripts to verify that services are running, check system load, or validate the availability of key processes. These automated checks play a crucial role in early detection of potential issues, triggering failover mechanisms or alerting administrators to investigate further. SSH's encrypted channels ensure that monitoring data collected during these operations remains secure and tamper-proof.

In cloud-based high-availability deployments, SSH is a vital tool for managing instances across multiple availability zones or regions. Whether working with AWS EC2 Auto Scaling Groups, Google Cloud's managed instance groups, or Azure Scale Sets, administrators use SSH to troubleshoot individual nodes that may encounter startup issues, configuration drift, or networking misconfigurations. SSH access ensures that system administrators can intervene rapidly, maintaining service uptime and reducing the risk of cascading failures across redundant systems.

Ultimately, SSH provides the operational flexibility, security, and reliability required to manage the complex environments that underpin high-availability architectures. Whether enabling direct system administration, supporting automation frameworks, or facilitating secure communication between critical components, SSH is deeply integrated into the workflows that keep modern infrastructure resilient. Its ubiquitous presence across platforms and environments makes it one of the most trusted tools for ensuring business continuity and high service availability, regardless of the size or complexity of the underlying infrastructure.

Troubleshooting SSH Connections

SSH is a highly reliable and secure protocol, but like any networking tool, users occasionally encounter issues when attempting to establish a connection. Troubleshooting SSH connections requires a systematic approach to diagnose and resolve problems that may arise due to configuration errors, network restrictions, authentication failures, or software bugs. Because SSH is often used in critical environments, gaining an in-depth understanding of the common factors that contribute to connection failures is essential for system administrators and IT professionals.

One of the most frequent causes of SSH connection issues is network reachability. Before analyzing SSH itself, administrators must first ensure that the client can reach the target server on the network. This often begins with simple tests such as using the ping command to check if the remote host is reachable. If the server does not respond to ping, it may be offline, located in a subnet with ICMP blocked, or behind a firewall that filters such traffic. Following ping tests, it is crucial to check that port 22—the default SSH port—is open and accessible. Tools such as telnet, nc (netcat), or nmap are commonly used to confirm whether port 22 is accepting connections. If the port is closed or filtered, it may be necessary to adjust firewall rules on either the server or intermediate networking devices.

Assuming the network path is clear, the next step involves verifying that the SSH service is running on the remote system. On most Linux and Unix-based systems, the SSH daemon (sshd) can be checked with systemctl status sshd or service sshd status. If the service is inactive or failed to start, reviewing the server's system logs, typically located in /var/log/auth.log or /var/log/secure, will often reveal why. Common issues include configuration syntax errors within the sshd_config file, missing dependencies, or conflicts with other services using the same port. Restarting the service after addressing any detected issues is necessary to restore normal operation.

Authentication failures are another prevalent cause of SSH connection problems. When a client attempts to connect to a server, it must present valid credentials in the form of a password or an SSH private key. If key-based authentication is used, mismatched or missing public keys on the server can result in access denial. Administrators should verify that the correct public key exists in the authorized_keys file of the target user account and that file permissions are properly set. Specifically, the .ssh directory should have 700 permissions, and the authorized_keys file should be set to 600. SSH is particularly strict about file permissions for security reasons, and overly permissive settings can prevent authentication from succeeding.

For password-based authentication, incorrect user credentials or password policies on the server may cause repeated login failures. Administrators should ensure that password authentication is enabled in the sshd_config file and that the user's password has not expired or been locked due to repeated failed login attempts. In environments with centralized authentication systems such as LDAP or Active Directory, connection issues could also stem from problems within those systems, such as expired credentials or network issues preventing the server from reaching the authentication provider.

Another layer of troubleshooting involves the SSH client itself. The ssh command-line tool provides detailed output when the -v flag is used, with additional verbosity enabled through -vv or -vvv. These flags reveal the step-by-step connection process, including hostname resolution, key exchange, authentication attempts, and any errors that occur. Reviewing this debug output often helps pinpoint whether the issue lies in the client configuration, network layer, or remote server.

In cases where DNS resolution is involved, it is important to ensure that the client is resolving the server's hostname to the correct IP address. Misconfigured DNS records or incorrect entries in /etc/hosts can cause SSH connections to fail silently or redirect to unintended destinations. The ssh client will also attempt to verify the server's host key against the known_hosts file. If the host key has changed—perhaps due to a server rebuild or an MITM attempt—the client will issue a warning and refuse to connect unless manually overridden. Administrators should validate the legitimacy of the host key change and remove or update the old entry in the known_hosts file as appropriate.

Port forwarding and NAT configurations can also introduce complexities when troubleshooting SSH connections. When servers reside behind network address translation (NAT) devices or load balancers, external clients may need to connect through forwarded ports or bastion hosts. Misconfigured NAT or port forwarding rules can result in timeout errors, dropped connections, or traffic being routed to the wrong internal resource. In these scenarios, confirming the end-to-end routing from the client to the destination server is critical.

Firewalls on both the client and server side can further complicate SSH access. Linux servers running iptables or nftables may have rules blocking inbound SSH connections, while enterprise-grade firewalls could restrict outbound SSH traffic from client networks. In some environments, network administrators implement strict egress filtering policies that prevent clients from initiating SSH sessions to unapproved external IP addresses. Adjusting firewall rules to allow SSH traffic while maintaining security best practices is an important balancing act during troubleshooting.

Connection stability issues, such as frequent disconnections or session freezes, may indicate deeper problems in the network path, such as packet loss, high latency, or MTU mismatches. SSH includes settings like ServerAliveInterval and ClientAliveInterval that can be adjusted to detect and handle dead connections more gracefully. These options instruct the client or server to send keepalive messages at regular intervals, preventing idle sessions from being prematurely closed by intermediate network devices.

Finally, troubleshooting SSH can extend into the realm of security appliances and intrusion detection or prevention systems. Some organizations deploy systems that actively monitor or block SSH traffic that exhibits suspicious patterns, such as high-frequency connection attempts or non-standard client behavior. When encountering intermittent or unexplained connection failures, administrators should consider whether security appliances are interfering with SSH sessions and coordinate with network security teams to whitelist trusted traffic where appropriate.

Troubleshooting SSH connections requires attention to every layer involved in the process—from client configurations and network paths to server settings and authentication mechanisms. A methodical approach that starts with basic connectivity checks and progresses through client and server diagnostics will often reveal the root cause of connection problems. By mastering SSH troubleshooting techniques, administrators are better equipped to maintain secure and stable remote access to critical infrastructure, even in the most complex and demanding environments.

SSH and Network Segmentation

Network segmentation is a core security strategy used to divide networks into smaller, isolated segments to limit lateral movement, reduce the attack surface, and improve traffic control. As modern infrastructures grow more complex and distributed, segmentation has become essential in protecting sensitive systems from unauthorized access and potential breaches. SSH plays a pivotal role within segmented network environments, acting as a secure gateway to access isolated systems while maintaining strict security and operational boundaries. Understanding how SSH integrates with segmentation policies is critical to achieving both operational efficiency and strong security controls.

At its core, SSH allows secure remote access to servers, switches, routers, and other critical infrastructure devices. In a flat network, SSH might provide direct access to any resource from any point on the network, increasing the risk of an attacker compromising one device and then pivoting freely to others. Network segmentation mitigates this risk by dividing the network into discrete security zones, each with its own access controls, firewall rules, and monitoring mechanisms. Segmentation limits where SSH traffic can originate and which systems can be reached, making it harder for malicious actors to escalate privileges or exfiltrate data.

One of the most common patterns for using SSH in segmented environments is the deployment of bastion hosts, also known as jump servers. A bastion host is strategically placed within a demilitarized zone (DMZ) or a secure subnet and serves as a controlled access point for administrators who need to SSH into deeper segments of the network. Rather than allowing direct SSH access to sensitive servers, firewalls are configured to permit SSH connections only to the bastion host, forcing all management traffic to flow through this monitored and secured checkpoint. SSH agent forwarding or ProxyCommand directives can then be used to establish onward connections from the bastion to internal resources.

In highly segmented architectures, such as those found in regulated industries like finance or healthcare, SSH is used in conjunction with strict firewall policies to control which users or services can access specific network segments. For instance, a network may be segmented into production, staging, and development environments, with access to the production segment limited to a small group of administrators. SSH allows these administrators to securely reach production servers without exposing them directly to the broader network or the internet. In such designs, access control lists (ACLs) and VLAN configurations are combined with SSH permissions to enforce both network-level and system-level isolation.

SSH also facilitates secure management of micro-segmented networks, where individual servers, containers, or applications are placed in their own isolated zones. Micro-segmentation, commonly implemented in cloud-native and zero trust environments, takes segmentation to a granular level. By isolating workloads down to the application or service level, organizations can tightly control east-west traffic and prevent unauthorized lateral movement. SSH supports this model by allowing secure, policy-enforced access to individual workloads. Bastion hosts, identity-aware proxies, or SSH jump configurations help administrators navigate from one micro-segment to another while adhering to strict access controls and audit requirements.

In segmented environments, SSH tunneling can serve both beneficial and potentially risky functions. Administrators frequently use SSH tunnels to forward traffic securely from their local systems to internal services that are otherwise inaccessible due to segmentation. For example, a database that resides in a secure zone might not be reachable from the administrator's workstation directly. However, an SSH tunnel established through a bastion host can securely forward traffic to the internal database service. While this enhances operational flexibility, it can also bypass network segmentation if not carefully controlled. To address this, security teams often disable or tightly regulate SSH port forwarding using the AllowTcpForwarding and PermitOpen directives in sshd_config files.

Logging and monitoring SSH activity is critical in segmented networks to ensure visibility and enforce compliance. SSH sessions that traverse network segments should be logged comprehensively, including source and destination IPs, usernames, timestamps, and executed commands. Centralized logging solutions can aggregate SSH logs from bastion hosts and internal systems, providing a holistic view of administrative activity across the entire network. In high-security environments, session recording tools may be deployed to capture full command histories and terminal outputs, enabling detailed audits of every SSH session that crosses network boundaries.

Another important aspect of using SSH in segmented networks is integrating with access management and authentication frameworks. Organizations often integrate SSH access with LDAP, Active Directory, or privileged access management (PAM) platforms, ensuring that authentication is not only tied to centralized user directories but also aligned with segmentation policies. For example, users who belong to a specific group in Active Directory may be granted SSH access to servers within the development segment but be prohibited from connecting to systems in the production zone. By leveraging SSH's support for key-based or certificate-based authentication in combination with these access policies, organizations can enforce fine-grained control over who can access each segment.

In hybrid and multi-cloud environments, SSH helps bridge segmented networks that span on-premises data centers and cloud providers. Enterprises often create dedicated VPN tunnels or direct connect links to securely connect cloud segments with on-premises infrastructure. SSH sessions traveling between these environments can leverage existing segmentation by routing through designated bastion hosts or secure gateways. By applying segmentation consistently across cloud and on-premises environments, organizations ensure that SSH traffic is appropriately routed, monitored, and controlled.

Network segmentation also plays a significant role in protecting critical infrastructure, such as industrial control systems (ICS) or supervisory control and data acquisition (SCADA) networks. These systems are commonly segmented from corporate IT networks to prevent exposure to internet-based threats. When administrators need to remotely manage ICS or SCADA devices, SSH is often used as the secure conduit, routed through carefully controlled gateways. In such scenarios, SSH serves not only as a remote access mechanism but also as a means of enforcing segmentation between sensitive operational technology (OT) networks and traditional IT systems.

Ultimately, SSH and network segmentation complement each other by providing layered defenses against unauthorized access and system compromise. By combining the strong encryption and authentication mechanisms of SSH with the compartmentalization and traffic controls of network segmentation, organizations create resilient and secure environments. SSH helps maintain operational agility, allowing secure management of segmented resources, while segmentation enforces structural boundaries that limit the potential impact of security incidents. Together, these strategies underpin a proactive approach to securing modern, distributed infrastructures.

SSH in Continuous Integration Pipelines

Continuous Integration (CI) pipelines are the backbone of modern software development workflows, automating the process of building, testing, and deploying code across environments. As development teams adopt CI practices to deliver software faster and with greater consistency, secure access to infrastructure becomes a critical requirement. SSH plays a central role in many CI pipelines, acting as the secure transport layer that allows automation tools to interact with remote servers, provision environments, deploy artifacts, and execute post-deployment tasks. Without SSH, automating the connection to and management of remote systems would be significantly more complex and less secure.

At the core of many CI pipelines is the need to connect from the CI server or runner to one or more target environments, which could include staging servers, production servers, cloud-based virtual machines, or container orchestration clusters. SSH enables this connection securely by providing encrypted communication and robust authentication mechanisms. Whether using Jenkins, GitLab CI, GitHub Actions, or other CI platforms, integrating SSH allows automated jobs to transfer files, execute remote commands, and configure services in a way that meets security best practices.

A common example of SSH in CI pipelines is during the deployment stage. After code is built and tested, a CI job may initiate an SSH session to a remote server to deploy application binaries, configuration files, or static assets. This can be done using a variety of techniques, such as copying files using SCP or SFTP, followed by running remote shell commands over SSH to start services, apply database migrations, or clear application caches. These steps are scripted and executed automatically every time code is committed, ensuring that deployments are repeatable, fast, and consistent.

SSH also plays a role in provisioning environments as part of infrastructure automation. For example, an Ansible playbook triggered by a CI pipeline will typically use SSH to connect to remote servers, configure operating system settings, install required software, and prepare the server to run the application. This automated provisioning allows teams to create and tear down environments on-demand, supporting ephemeral infrastructure and reducing the risk of configuration drift. The security provided by SSH ensures that the provisioning process does not expose sensitive information such as credentials or infrastructure secrets.

In more advanced CI workflows, SSH enables pipelines to interact with multiple environments or services during the same pipeline execution. For instance, a pipeline might connect to a staging environment to run integration tests against a fully deployed application before promoting the code to production. The CI system will initiate SSH connections to deploy the application to staging, trigger test scripts, collect logs, and evaluate results before deciding whether to proceed with deployment to the next environment. By automating these actions with SSH, organizations reduce manual intervention and accelerate delivery cycles.

A major consideration when using SSH in CI pipelines is secure key management. Since CI jobs are automated, they cannot manually input passwords or passphrases for SSH authentication. Instead, SSH key pairs are generated specifically for the CI system, with the private key securely stored in encrypted secrets vaults, environment variables, or

CI tool credential managers. The corresponding public key is deployed to the authorized_keys file of the target servers, allowing the CI runner to authenticate non-interactively. This setup must be carefully secured to prevent unauthorized access. Private keys should never be hardcoded into scripts or exposed in logs, and access to the CI platform itself must be tightly controlled.

Some organizations take key security a step further by using SSH certificates instead of static keys. In this model, the CI pipeline retrieves short-lived SSH certificates from a trusted certificate authority as part of its workflow. These certificates are valid for a limited time and can specify precise roles, host restrictions, and command constraints. Using SSH certificates reduces the risk of key compromise and ensures that even if a certificate is exposed, it will quickly expire and become unusable.

SSH port forwarding is another valuable feature in CI pipelines. Port forwarding allows a pipeline to securely access services that are not publicly exposed, such as internal APIs, databases, or admin interfaces located behind a firewall or on a private network. For example, a CI job may establish an SSH tunnel to forward traffic from the CI runner to a database in a restricted environment, allowing tests or migration scripts to run securely. This eliminates the need to expose sensitive services to the internet while still enabling automation workflows to interact with them.

In Kubernetes-centric workflows, SSH can be used by CI pipelines to manage underlying infrastructure that hosts container orchestration clusters. While Kubernetes itself is typically managed via APIs and kubectl, there are often scenarios where SSH access is needed to interact directly with nodes for maintenance, debugging, or configuring services such as ingress controllers and monitoring agents. In hybrid architectures where clusters span cloud and on-premises systems, SSH provides the secure bridge for pipelines to manage infrastructure components that lie outside the Kubernetes API's scope.

SSH also supports CI workflows that include rollback mechanisms. When a deployment fails due to a misconfiguration or an application error, the pipeline can automatically SSH into the affected environment, revert to a previous release, and restart services to restore availability. These rollback scripts ensure that recovery processes are executed quickly and consistently, minimizing downtime and service disruption.

In addition to deployments, SSH is frequently used in CI pipelines for tasks such as log collection, metric extraction, and system health checks. Pipelines may SSH into target systems to gather application logs, system metrics, or performance data, and then aggregate the information for reporting or post-deployment validation. This step helps teams ensure that deployments meet performance benchmarks and do not introduce regressions into the production environment.

While SSH provides powerful capabilities for automating CI pipelines, it must be coupled with rigorous monitoring and auditing practices. SSH sessions initiated by CI jobs should be logged at both the CI platform and target server levels, providing a complete audit trail of automated access and actions. Logs should be reviewed regularly for anomalies, such as unauthorized SSH attempts, unexpected commands, or unusual connection patterns.

SSH remains a critical enabler of secure and automated CI pipelines. It ensures that the automation of deployment, provisioning, and testing processes can occur across distributed environments while maintaining strong encryption, authentication, and access controls. Whether in traditional server-based deployments, hybrid cloud architectures, or cloud-native applications, SSH continues to empower teams to automate with confidence while adhering to security best practices.

SSH Honeypots for Threat Detection

SSH honeypots are a powerful and deceptive security strategy used to detect, analyze, and mitigate threats targeting remote access services. In a landscape where attackers continually scan for vulnerable SSH servers to exploit, honeypots act as bait, deliberately exposing an SSH service that appears to be a legitimate target but is designed to attract and trap malicious actors. These decoy systems gather intelligence on attack techniques, tools, and behavior while protecting production infrastructure by diverting attackers' attention away from real assets. SSH honeypots have become a critical component in proactive threat detection strategies, enabling organizations to stay ahead of evolving threats.

An SSH honeypot typically mimics a fully functioning SSH server, complete with an open port, a familiar banner, and seemingly standard login prompts. However, behind the scenes, it operates under controlled conditions where all interactions are logged, analyzed, and contained. These honeypots can be deployed in various configurations, ranging from low-interaction setups that simply log brute-force attempts to high-interaction honeypots that simulate an entire operating system environment, providing attackers with a convincing but fake system to explore. Regardless of the sophistication, the primary goal is to collect actionable intelligence on threat actors without exposing sensitive systems to actual risk.

One of the most common attack patterns observed in SSH honeypots is brute-force login attempts. Automated bots and scripts scour the internet looking for open SSH ports, systematically attempting username and password combinations in the hope of gaining unauthorized access. By running an SSH honeypot and capturing these login attempts, security teams can identify common password patterns, credential lists, and targeted usernames that may be relevant to their actual systems. This intelligence helps improve password policies and informs defensive strategies by revealing which usernames and password combinations are most frequently targeted.

Beyond brute-force attempts, SSH honeypots also capture more advanced techniques employed by attackers once initial access is gained. For example, high-interaction honeypots allow attackers to move past the login phase and execute commands in a sandboxed environment. This reveals the tools and tactics used during the post-exploitation phase, such as privilege escalation attempts, malware deployment, lateral movement strategies, or the creation of backdoor accounts. Capturing these behaviors in a controlled environment provides deep insight into attacker methodologies and can be used to strengthen defenses against real intrusions.

Honeypots also serve as an early warning system. The presence of repeated or highly targeted SSH attacks against a honeypot may indicate a broader campaign or a focused reconnaissance effort against the organization's infrastructure. Security teams can respond by tightening firewall rules, blocking offending IP addresses, and applying additional layers of monitoring and hardening to production servers. In some cases, intelligence gathered from a honeypot may reveal previously unknown attacker infrastructure, such as command-and-control servers or malware repositories, which can be shared with the wider security community to disrupt ongoing threat campaigns.

SSH honeypots can also detect the use of custom malware or automated attack frameworks that are difficult to identify through traditional security tools. By allowing adversaries to deploy their toolkits in the honeypot's environment, security teams can capture binaries, scripts, and payloads for detailed analysis. This provides valuable indicators of compromise (IOCs) such as file hashes, domain names, and IP addresses, which can be incorporated into threat intelligence feeds and used to bolster intrusion detection and prevention systems.

Deployment strategies for SSH honeypots vary depending on the goals of the organization. Low-interaction honeypots, such as Cowrie, are widely used for collecting SSH brute-force attempts and basic command input. These honeypots emulate an SSH service and present a fake shell to attackers while logging every keystroke and connection detail. Because they are lightweight and simple to configure, they can be deployed widely across an organization's network perimeter or cloud environments without introducing significant resource overhead. High-interaction honeypots, such as those running actual virtual machines, provide a more convincing environment but require stronger isolation and monitoring due to the increased risk associated with allowing attackers to interact with a real operating system.

To ensure that SSH honeypots remain effective and do not endanger production systems, strict containment and monitoring policies must be enforced. Honeypots should be segmented from the organization's operational network using firewalls, VLANs, or isolated virtual private clouds (VPCs). Outbound traffic from the honeypot should be restricted or logged to prevent the system from being used as a pivot point to launch attacks on other targets. Additionally, honeypots should be closely monitored with alerting systems configured to notify security teams of suspicious behavior in real time.

The use of SSH honeypots is also valuable in understanding attacker motivations and objectives. By analyzing patterns in commands, downloaded payloads, or exfiltration attempts, organizations can infer whether attackers are opportunistic script kiddies, professional cybercriminals, or state-sponsored actors. For instance, some attackers may focus on deploying cryptocurrency miners on compromised systems, while others may attempt to install rootkits, steal data, or use the server as part of a botnet. These insights help organizations refine their threat models and allocate resources to counter the most relevant risks.

Integrating SSH honeypots into a broader security monitoring and response strategy enhances their effectiveness. Logs and alerts from honeypots can feed directly into Security Information and Event Management (SIEM) platforms, enabling correlation with other security events across the network. This holistic view helps detect attack patterns that span beyond the honeypot and affect other parts of the infrastructure. Honeypot data can also complement threat hunting activities by guiding analysts toward anomalous behaviors or previously undetected footholds.

SSH honeypots are not just defensive tools but also research platforms that contribute to global cybersecurity awareness. Many organizations participate in collaborative initiatives, sharing honeypot data with academic institutions, security researchers, and industry groups. This collaboration helps improve the collective understanding of cyber threats and informs the development of new detection techniques and countermeasures.

SSH honeypots are a crucial component of modern threat detection and intelligence-gathering strategies. By simulating vulnerable targets and luring attackers into controlled environments, organizations can gain invaluable insights into attacker behavior, techniques, and infrastructure. When combined with strong isolation measures and integrated with broader security monitoring frameworks, SSH honeypots serve as a powerful force multiplier for defending against an increasingly sophisticated threat landscape.

Future Trends: SSH and Quantum Computing

The advancement of quantum computing is poised to disrupt many of the cryptographic systems currently securing digital communications, including the SSH protocol. SSH relies heavily on public key cryptography to authenticate users and protect sessions against eavesdropping, man-in-the-middle attacks, and unauthorized access. Today's algorithms, such as RSA, DSA, and ECDSA, are secure under the assumption that adversaries only possess classical computing capabilities. However, the emergence of quantum computers capable of executing Shor's algorithm threatens to render these encryption methods obsolete by solving the underlying mathematical problems, like integer factorization and discrete logarithms, exponentially faster than classical machines.

This looming shift has prompted the cybersecurity community to explore how SSH and similar protocols will need to evolve to remain secure in a post-quantum world. Quantum computers of sufficient scale and reliability are still under development, but it is widely accepted that they will eventually be able to break many of the cryptographic primitives currently in use. The anticipated timeline for this disruptive capability varies, but organizations and governments are already taking steps to prepare, recognizing the long-term value of data and the potential for attackers to harvest encrypted traffic today and decrypt it in the future using quantum resources, a threat referred to as harvest now, decrypt later.

SSH's reliance on algorithms like RSA and ECDSA places it squarely within the realm of cryptographic systems vulnerable to quantum attacks. This means that any data or authentication credentials exchanged during an SSH session using these algorithms could be compromised if intercepted today and stored until quantum computing matures. Forward secrecy, achieved through ephemeral

Diffie-Hellman key exchanges, mitigates some of this risk by ensuring session keys are transient and not dependent on long-term secrets. However, even these methods can be weakened by quantum algorithms that efficiently solve the discrete logarithm problem.

To address these challenges, the cryptography and open-source communities are working toward the integration of quantum-resistant algorithms into widely used protocols, including SSH. The National Institute of Standards and Technology (NIST) has been leading an initiative to identify and standardize post-quantum cryptographic algorithms that rely on hard problems assumed to be resistant to quantum attacks, such as lattice-based, hash-based, and code-based schemes. These algorithms are being carefully vetted for both their security properties and their practical performance in real-world applications.

For SSH, this shift will likely result in a gradual transition to hybrid models where classical algorithms are combined with quantum-resistant primitives to provide both backward compatibility and enhanced security. OpenSSH, the most widely used implementation of SSH, has already begun to experiment with quantum-safe key exchange mechanisms. For example, support for the NTRUEncrypt and Streamlined NTRU Prime algorithms, which are lattice-based and designed to resist quantum attacks, has been added in experimental form to OpenSSH releases. These hybrid schemes allow SSH sessions to use both traditional and post-quantum key exchanges, providing security even if one of the components is later found to be vulnerable.

The evolution of SSH in a post-quantum era will also require careful consideration of performance and operational implications. Many post-quantum algorithms introduce larger key sizes and more computational overhead compared to current cryptographic standards. In resource-constrained environments, such as IoT devices or embedded systems, adopting these algorithms could present challenges related to memory usage, latency, and bandwidth consumption. SSH clients and servers will need to balance these trade-offs to ensure secure, efficient connections without compromising usability.

Another area of research focuses on developing entirely new protocols or extensions to SSH that natively support quantum-resistant algorithms, rather than relying on hybrid approaches. As these protocols are formalized and tested, industry-wide adoption will depend on interoperability between SSH clients and servers, as well as compatibility with existing infrastructure, such as automated scripts, configuration management tools, and monitoring systems. The transition to post-quantum SSH will require updates to software, configuration policies, and key management practices.

Key management will play a critical role in the secure deployment of post-quantum SSH. Organizations must prepare to rotate and replace existing SSH keys and certificates with post-quantum equivalents. This migration will likely occur over several years, depending on regulatory pressures, industry best practices, and the progress of quantum computing advancements. Additionally, security teams will need to educate users on new key formats, implement updated automation pipelines, and adapt CI/CD processes to accommodate new cryptographic requirements.

SSH's future in the quantum era will also be shaped by legal and regulatory factors. Governments and industry groups are already developing guidelines to ensure that critical infrastructure, financial systems, and sensitive data are protected against quantum threats. Sectors such as defense, finance, and healthcare will be among the first to adopt post-quantum cryptography, given their heightened risk profiles and the long-term sensitivity of the data they manage.

Furthermore, as quantum technologies mature, the security of SSH sessions will increasingly depend on multi-layered defenses that go beyond cryptography. Techniques such as network segmentation, access controls, and continuous monitoring will continue to play essential roles in securing remote access workflows. Even as SSH evolves to include quantum-safe algorithms, organizations must maintain a defense-in-depth strategy to mitigate both quantum and classical threats.

Looking ahead, organizations that rely heavily on SSH for secure remote access, automation, and system administration should start planning for a post-quantum transition now. This includes staying informed about advancements in quantum computing, monitoring the NIST post-quantum standardization process, and testing quantum-resistant SSH implementations as they become available. Forward-thinking security teams are already deploying pilot projects that evaluate hybrid key exchange models and assess the performance impact of integrating post-quantum algorithms into existing workflows.

While quantum computing introduces uncertainty into the security landscape, it also drives innovation and resilience in protocols like SSH. The cryptographic community's proactive efforts to adapt SSH for the quantum future will ensure that it remains a trusted and indispensable tool for secure communications in the decades to come. As with past cryptographic shifts, collaboration between researchers, developers, and industry stakeholders will be essential to navigating this transition smoothly and ensuring that SSH continues to protect sensitive information against both emerging and traditional threats.

SSH Alternatives: When and Why

While SSH is widely regarded as the gold standard for secure remote access and encrypted communications between systems, there are scenarios where alternative tools and protocols may be better suited for specific use cases. SSH has long been the backbone of remote administration, automation, and secure file transfers, yet it is not always the optimal solution for every environment. As networks, workflows, and security requirements evolve, organizations may find that alternatives to SSH can provide improved performance, simplicity, or specialized functionality tailored to their unique operational needs. Understanding when and why to consider SSH alternatives is essential for selecting the right tool for a given task.

One notable alternative to SSH is the Remote Desktop Protocol (RDP), which is primarily used in Windows environments to provide graphical remote access to servers and workstations. While SSH excels at command-line-based administration of Linux and Unix systems, RDP enables users to interact with a full graphical desktop remotely. This makes RDP particularly useful for system administrators who need to manage Windows servers, perform tasks within GUI-based applications, or provide remote technical support to end-users. However, RDP has historically faced security challenges, such as vulnerability to brute-force attacks and a history of critical vulnerabilities. As a result, organizations must harden RDP deployments with multi-factor authentication, strong password policies, and network segmentation to mitigate risks.

Another alternative that is often discussed in the context of remote access is Virtual Network Computing (VNC). VNC provides cross-platform graphical access to remote systems and is commonly used in development environments, educational settings, and remote support scenarios. Unlike SSH, which focuses on secure shell access, VNC mirrors the graphical display of the remote machine and allows users to control the keyboard and mouse as if they were physically present. While convenient, VNC is less secure in its default configuration as it does not natively encrypt traffic. Administrators who choose VNC must tunnel sessions through SSH or use versions that support TLS encryption to ensure secure operation.

For file transfers specifically, some organizations may opt for alternatives such as FTPS (FTP Secure) or HTTPS-based file upload mechanisms instead of SCP or SFTP, which rely on SSH. FTPS adds SSL/TLS encryption to the traditional FTP protocol, providing a secure option for file transfers in environments where legacy systems or existing workflows require FTP compatibility. Similarly, web-based applications that facilitate file uploads via HTTPS offer simplicity and user-friendliness for non-technical staff who may not be familiar with command-line tools like SFTP.

When it comes to remote command execution and automation in large-scale cloud environments, cloud-native tools such as AWS Systems Manager Session Manager, Azure Bastion, or Google Cloud's OS Login are gaining traction as SSH alternatives. These services integrate tightly with cloud provider identity and access management systems, allowing administrators to initiate secure shell sessions or run commands on virtual machines without exposing SSH ports to the internet. These tools reduce the reliance on traditional SSH key management by integrating access control with cloud-native policies and logging mechanisms, simplifying compliance efforts and improving security posture in public cloud environments.

Additionally, Zero Trust Network Access (ZTNA) solutions are emerging as modern alternatives to traditional SSH for secure remote access. ZTNA platforms, such as Google BeyondCorp or Cloudflare Access, adopt a model where trust is not granted based on network location alone but is continually verified based on user identity, device posture, and contextual data. These solutions often replace traditional VPN and SSH bastion host setups by offering secure web portals or identity-aware proxies that facilitate access to internal applications and services. ZTNA tools may reduce the need for direct SSH access in environments where remote users only need to interact with specific services rather than administering full servers.

In highly regulated industries or organizations subject to stringent compliance requirements, Privileged Access Management (PAM) solutions provide secure alternatives to SSH by offering session brokering, credential vaulting, and granular access control. Solutions such as CyberArk, BeyondTrust, and Thycotic Secret Server integrate with PAM systems to limit direct SSH access and replace it with controlled, audited sessions. In these setups, users request access through the PAM platform, which injects credentials and initiates sessions without exposing private keys or passwords to the user. This reduces the risk of credential misuse and improves oversight over privileged operations.

There are also situations where SSH may not be the best option due to performance concerns. In scenarios where ultra-low latency is critical, such as high-frequency trading or scientific computing, protocols that offer lighter encryption or faster handshake mechanisms may be preferred. Some organizations may use lightweight remote shell tools like Mosh (Mobile Shell), which is designed to improve performance over high-latency or unreliable connections. Mosh uses UDP rather than TCP and maintains session persistence even when network connectivity is intermittent, making it a useful alternative for mobile users or remote locations with unstable internet access.

In highly constrained embedded systems or IoT environments, where computing resources and bandwidth are limited, SSH's overhead may be too heavy. In such cases, developers might opt for simpler remote management protocols such as Telnet, despite its lack of native encryption, or proprietary lightweight agents designed specifically for embedded devices. When using less secure alternatives like Telnet, it is essential to mitigate risks by restricting network exposure, using VPNs or SSH tunnels, and limiting the command scope to minimize the attack surface.

The decision to use an SSH alternative is often influenced by specific technical requirements, user experience considerations, and broader security architecture. For example, in environments where user convenience is paramount, graphical tools like RDP or VNC may offer a more intuitive interface than command-line SSH sessions. Conversely, highly automated cloud-native infrastructures may lean toward API-driven or identity-integrated solutions that reduce dependency on direct SSH access altogether.

Ultimately, while SSH remains an essential tool for secure remote administration, it is not a one-size-fits-all solution. The landscape of remote access, file transfer, and automation tools continues to evolve, driven by advancements in cloud computing, security models, and user expectations. Evaluating when and why to consider SSH alternatives requires a careful assessment of operational needs, threat models, and regulatory environments. Organizations benefit most when they select the right tool for each use case, balancing usability, security, and scalability to meet their unique infrastructure and business requirements.

Building a Secure SSH Gateway

An SSH gateway, also commonly referred to as a jump host or bastion server, is a critical component in modern secure infrastructure design. It acts as a controlled entry point through which administrators and automation tools can access internal or segmented networks. By funneling SSH traffic through a single, hardened gateway, organizations can reduce attack surfaces, centralize access control, and enforce auditing of remote sessions. Building a secure SSH gateway is more than just deploying a virtual machine with SSH enabled; it requires meticulous configuration, integration with identity and access management systems, and ongoing monitoring to ensure it serves its purpose without introducing additional risks.

The first step in building a secure SSH gateway is selecting a suitable host system. Many organizations deploy the gateway in a demilitarized zone (DMZ) or a dedicated subnet designed to bridge external networks with internal segments securely. The underlying operating system should be minimal, often a stripped-down Linux distribution, to reduce unnecessary services and vulnerabilities. The fewer applications and daemons running on the gateway, the smaller the attack surface, and the easier it is to maintain security. Regular updates and patching schedules must be enforced to ensure the gateway remains resilient to newly discovered threats.

SSH hardening on the gateway is fundamental to its security. Password-based authentication should be disabled in favor of key-based or certificate-based authentication. Allowing only SSH public key authentication mitigates the risk of brute-force attacks and reduces the chances of credential theft. The sshd_config file should be configured to disable root login, enforce strong ciphers and key exchange algorithms, and restrict SSH agent and TCP forwarding where not explicitly required. Additional SSH options like setting a short ClientAliveInterval and ClientAliveCountMax can help close idle or abandoned sessions, limiting the window of opportunity for session hijacking.

Controlling who can access the SSH gateway is another crucial element. Integration with centralized identity and access management (IAM) systems such as LDAP, Active Directory, or cloud-native IAM services ensures that access policies are consistent across the organization. For even tighter security, multi-factor authentication (MFA) can be enforced on the gateway itself, requiring users to provide a second factor, such as a time-based one-time password (TOTP) or hardware security key, before being granted access.

Network-level protections must also be in place. Firewalls should be configured to allow SSH traffic to the gateway only from trusted IP ranges, such as corporate VPN endpoints or specific administrator workstations. Outbound traffic from the gateway should be limited to the necessary internal subnets, minimizing the risk that a compromised gateway could be used as a pivot point for lateral movement within the network. In more advanced configurations, security groups or virtual network rules can be used to enforce segmentation dynamically.

Session logging and monitoring are essential for detecting anomalies and maintaining an audit trail of administrative activities. Every SSH session passing through the gateway should be logged with sufficient detail, capturing user identities, source IP addresses, session timestamps, and executed commands. Centralized log aggregation and analysis tools such as ELK Stack, Splunk, or cloud-native logging services can be used to collect and monitor gateway logs in real-time. For organizations with strict compliance requirements, session recording tools that capture the full terminal output can be deployed to provide a forensic record of each session.

For automation and DevOps workflows, it is common to configure the SSH gateway to act as a proxy. The ProxyJump or ProxyCommand options in the SSH client configuration file allow users and scripts to automatically route connections through the gateway without requiring manual steps. This facilitates secure and seamless access to internal systems from external networks while preserving the security benefits of a centralized gateway. Automation tools such as Ansible, Terraform, or Jenkins can be configured to leverage the gateway as a jump point when deploying applications, managing infrastructure, or executing remote commands.

Another security enhancement is implementing just-in-time (JIT) access models on the SSH gateway. JIT access ensures that accounts are granted temporary SSH permissions for a limited duration, reducing the standing privileges of users and decreasing the attack surface. This model can be combined with access request workflows, where users must submit access requests that are reviewed and approved before temporary credentials or certificates are provisioned.

In cloud-native environments, organizations increasingly deploy SSH gateways as ephemeral resources. Rather than maintaining a persistent bastion host, ephemeral gateways are spun up on-demand using infrastructure-as-code (IaC) tools and terminated after the required access window has closed. This reduces the exposure time of the gateway to the internet and minimizes the risks associated with long-lived infrastructure.

An additional best practice is to enable SSH connection multiplexing for users and automation pipelines connecting through the gateway. Connection multiplexing allows multiple SSH sessions to share a single TCP connection, reducing authentication overhead and improving performance when running multiple tasks across internal systems through the gateway.

The concept of defense in depth applies strongly to SSH gateways. While the gateway itself is a critical security control, it should not be treated as the sole protective layer. Internal systems behind the gateway must also be hardened individually, with their own access controls, logging, and monitoring configurations. Furthermore, integrating the SSH gateway into the organization's security incident and event management (SIEM) and security operations workflows ensures that suspicious or unauthorized activities can be detected and responded to quickly.

Finally, user training is vital to the successful operation of a secure SSH gateway. Administrators and developers who use the gateway should be well-versed in secure SSH usage practices, such as safeguarding private keys, understanding MFA requirements, and avoiding unsafe configurations like port forwarding without approval. Regular security reviews and access audits should be conducted to ensure that access permissions are current and follow the principle of least privilege.

Building a secure SSH gateway requires a combination of technical configurations, policy enforcement, and operational discipline. When implemented correctly, an SSH gateway becomes a key pillar of secure remote access infrastructure, protecting internal resources while enabling efficient and auditable administrative operations. It serves as both a security control and an operational enabler, ensuring that remote access remains both flexible and secure in modern IT environments.

Real-World SSH Incident Case Studies

SSH is a critical tool in securing and managing servers, but when misconfigured or improperly secured, it can become a vector for significant security incidents. Real-world cases involving SSH illustrate both its importance and the potential consequences of failing to implement best practices. These case studies highlight incidents where SSH was exploited by attackers, as well as scenarios where SSH served as a critical component in mitigating damage during security breaches.

One of the most notable SSH-related incidents occurred at a large hosting provider where attackers gained unauthorized access to customer servers through weak SSH key management practices. In this incident, attackers compromised the SSH private key of a system administrator whose key was reused across multiple servers. Once the attackers obtained the key, they were able to bypass traditional password authentication and gain access to a significant number of internal systems. The breach was exacerbated by the fact that no key rotation policy was in place, and stale keys from former employees remained active in authorized_keys files across hundreds of production servers. The attackers used their foothold to deploy cryptocurrency mining malware, consuming significant system resources and impacting service availability for numerous customers. This case served as a wake-up call for the organization, prompting them to implement centralized SSH key management, enforce key rotation, and audit all keys to ensure proper access controls.

Another high-profile incident involved a research university where an unsecured SSH service became the target of a persistent brute-force attack. The attackers systematically attempted thousands of password combinations on an exposed SSH port over several weeks. Eventually, they successfully authenticated to a non-critical but overlooked system using default credentials that were never changed after initial deployment. Once inside, the attackers escalated privileges using a known vulnerability in the operating system and pivoted laterally across the internal network, eventually reaching research servers containing valuable proprietary data. The investigation revealed that the organization lacked proper SSH hardening measures, such as disabling password authentication, enforcing key-based access, and restricting SSH access to trusted IP addresses. Following this incident, the university adopted a zero-trust approach, implemented bastion hosts for segmented network access, and deployed intrusion detection systems to identify future brute-force activity.

In the financial sector, a major bank faced an SSH-related incident where an attacker leveraged a compromised SSH key to infiltrate a critical internal system. The attacker was able to escalate privileges and exfiltrate sensitive customer data, resulting in regulatory scrutiny and reputational damage. Post-incident analysis showed that SSH access logs were not being forwarded to a centralized logging platform, and no alerts were triggered during the initial stages of the breach. By the time the security team became aware of unusual system behavior, the data had already been exfiltrated through encrypted SSH tunnels. This case highlighted the importance of real-time monitoring and auditing of SSH sessions, especially in regulated environments where financial and personal data are involved. The bank responded by integrating SSH session monitoring into its SIEM system, enabling better visibility and faster response times to unusual SSH activity.

In contrast, there are also examples where SSH served as a vital defensive tool during security breaches. In one incident at a global technology company, attackers launched a ransomware campaign against the organization's infrastructure, encrypting data on several servers and demanding a ransom. However, the security team used SSH as a secure communication channel to access unaffected systems, isolate compromised machines, and coordinate recovery efforts. SSH tunnels were used to securely transfer clean backups from off-site locations to restore critical systems without relying on exposed network services. The secure and encrypted nature of SSH provided a reliable method for incident response teams to execute recovery procedures without the risk of attackers intercepting communications or sabotaging recovery operations.

A unique incident occurred in a cloud service provider where automated infrastructure deployment tools were configured to expose SSH ports on all newly provisioned instances by default. Attackers conducting routine scans identified exposed development and staging servers that were intended to remain private. Using brute-force techniques, attackers gained access to several cloud instances and deployed lightweight cryptocurrency miners, causing financial losses due to inflated compute usage costs. The incident was traced back to misconfigured infrastructure-as-code templates that failed to properly apply security group rules limiting SSH access. The provider subsequently updated deployment pipelines to enforce network segmentation, required all instances to default to closed SSH ports unless explicitly needed, and conducted thorough reviews of all automated provisioning scripts.

In another case, a telecommunications company discovered that third-party contractors had retained persistent SSH keys on production servers even after their projects had been completed. During a routine security audit, it was found that several keys remained active for months beyond the contractors' engagement period. While no malicious activity was detected, the organization recognized the risk of potential insider threats or credential theft leading to a breach. This led to the implementation of an automated system that tied SSH key expiration to contract durations, ensuring that third-party access was removed promptly after project completion.

One final case involved a sophisticated attack against a government agency where an advanced persistent threat (APT) group leveraged SSH as a covert channel for data exfiltration. The attackers initially compromised a public-facing web server and planted malware that established outbound SSH tunnels to command-and-control infrastructure. By routing traffic through these encrypted tunnels, the attackers were able to exfiltrate sensitive documents over several months without detection, as traditional perimeter defenses did not inspect SSH-encrypted traffic. The agency's security team eventually detected anomalies in outbound network traffic volumes, leading to the discovery of the SSH tunnels. The investigation underscored the importance of inspecting and monitoring encrypted traffic leaving the network, as well as segmenting sensitive systems to prevent the establishment of such tunnels.

These real-world case studies demonstrate that while SSH is a powerful security tool, it can also become an attack vector if mismanaged or left unmonitored. The recurring themes across these incidents highlight the importance of key management, session logging, network segmentation, and continuous monitoring. Properly securing SSH requires not just technical configurations, but also process discipline and organizational awareness to ensure that access controls remain aligned with evolving threats and operational needs. As these cases show, SSH can either strengthen or weaken an organization's security posture depending on how effectively it is deployed and managed.

SSH in Industrial Control Systems (ICS)

Industrial Control Systems (ICS) are critical components of national infrastructure and essential services, responsible for managing processes in sectors such as energy, manufacturing, water treatment, and transportation. These systems include Supervisory Control and Data Acquisition (SCADA) platforms, Programmable Logic Controllers (PLCs), and Distributed Control Systems (DCS). While traditionally isolated from corporate IT networks and the internet, the increasing adoption of modern technologies and remote access requirements has led to a convergence of IT and OT (Operational Technology) environments. As this convergence accelerates, Secure Shell (SSH) has emerged as a vital tool for administrators and engineers to securely manage and troubleshoot ICS environments, bringing both benefits and challenges.

SSH provides encrypted, authenticated remote access to systems controlling industrial processes, enabling secure communication over untrusted networks. In environments where remote maintenance, diagnostics, or updates are necessary, SSH ensures that sensitive data and control commands are not exposed to eavesdropping or interception. Many ICS vendors have integrated SSH into modern hardware and software platforms, allowing administrators to access devices such as Human-Machine Interfaces (HMIs), industrial routers, and edge gateways remotely. This capability is crucial in industries where remote sites, such as oil rigs or wind farms, may be located in geographically isolated areas where physical access is costly or time-consuming.

Despite these advantages, the use of SSH within ICS environments must be approached with caution due to the unique security and operational requirements of OT systems. Unlike IT environments, where systems can often be patched and rebooted regularly, ICS components may operate in real-time or near-real-time conditions, controlling critical infrastructure where downtime is unacceptable. The potential for human error or cyberattacks exploiting remote access mechanisms is magnified in these settings, where the consequences could include operational disruption, physical damage, or safety incidents.

To mitigate risks, SSH implementations in ICS environments should be part of a carefully designed security strategy that adheres to ICS-specific best practices. Network segmentation is one of the most important principles in securing ICS networks, and SSH must be used in alignment with these boundaries. Control networks should be segmented from corporate IT networks, with SSH access restricted to designated jump hosts or bastion servers located in DMZs. These controlled access points allow engineers and administrators to reach industrial systems securely while enforcing centralized auditing and monitoring of SSH sessions.

Key management is another crucial consideration. In many ICS environments, legacy practices such as shared administrator credentials or static passwords have historically been common. The introduction of SSH provides an opportunity to modernize authentication workflows by implementing key-based authentication. Administrators should use strong SSH keys or certificates for authentication, eliminating reliance on weak or reused passwords. In addition, SSH keys must be rotated regularly, and access should be revoked promptly when personnel leave the organization or change roles.

ICS environments must also implement strict control over SSH forwarding capabilities. Features such as SSH tunneling and agent forwarding, while useful in IT settings, can create security blind spots if misused in OT networks. To reduce the risk of unauthorized lateral movement or data exfiltration, SSH servers in ICS environments should be configured to disable unnecessary forwarding options. PermitOpen directives can be used to strictly define which ports or destinations are allowed for SSH tunnels when absolutely necessary, ensuring that remote access is tightly scoped and controlled.

Another layer of protection involves logging and auditing SSH activity within ICS networks. Given the critical nature of industrial processes, every SSH session must be logged in detail, including information about the user, source IP address, session duration, and executed commands. These logs should be collected and forwarded to centralized security information and event management (SIEM) platforms for real-time monitoring and alerting. This enables security teams to detect and respond to suspicious behavior, such as unauthorized access attempts, privilege escalation activities, or anomalous commands issued to industrial devices.

SSH plays a crucial role during incident response and disaster recovery efforts in ICS environments. In the event of a cyberattack or system failure, remote SSH access enables responders to isolate affected devices, deploy patches or configuration changes, and restore functionality with minimal delay. This is especially important for organizations that operate critical infrastructure under regulatory obligations requiring rapid recovery and incident reporting. The encrypted nature of SSH ensures that incident response activities are conducted securely, even over potentially compromised networks.

The adoption of SSH in ICS environments also intersects with regulatory frameworks and industry standards. Guidelines such as the NIST Cybersecurity Framework, IEC 62443, and NERC CIP emphasize the need for secure remote access mechanisms, access control, and system hardening within critical infrastructure sectors. Organizations leveraging SSH must align their practices with these standards, implementing technical and administrative controls to mitigate cyber risks. This includes enforcing least privilege access, segmenting networks, conducting regular security assessments, and documenting remote access procedures.

Vendor-specific implementations of SSH on industrial devices require careful consideration. Many ICS components may ship with SSH services enabled by default, but with outdated firmware, weak default credentials, or permissive configurations. Organizations must audit all connected devices to ensure that SSH services are configured securely, unnecessary services are disabled, and firmware is kept up to date. When industrial devices lack the capacity to support modern SSH configurations securely, compensating controls such as network-based firewalls or application layer gateways should be deployed to protect these systems from unauthorized SSH access.

In some advanced ICS environments, organizations are beginning to integrate SSH access with centralized identity and access management platforms. By linking SSH authentication to corporate directory services, such as Active Directory or LDAP, administrators can enforce role-based access control and multi-factor authentication for ICS systems. This helps to ensure that only authorized personnel with a legitimate business need can access critical devices through SSH, while reducing administrative overhead associated with managing local accounts on each device.

While SSH introduces essential capabilities for secure remote administration in ICS networks, its deployment must be tailored to the unique operational constraints and security requirements of OT environments. Improperly configured or poorly monitored SSH access could inadvertently increase risk rather than reduce it. Therefore, collaboration between IT security teams and OT engineers is vital to developing policies and practices that balance operational uptime with security best practices.

SSH has become a key enabler of modern ICS management, allowing organizations to maintain, monitor, and recover industrial systems efficiently. However, realizing the full benefits of SSH in this context requires disciplined implementation, robust controls, and ongoing vigilance to ensure that remote access remains secure, auditable, and aligned with the specialized demands of industrial control environments.

SSH for Secure API Access

SSH is traditionally associated with remote shell access and secure file transfers, but it also plays an important role in enabling secure API access, particularly in complex and highly regulated environments. As modern infrastructures rely heavily on APIs to connect systems, automate workflows, and expose services both internally and externally, securing these interfaces has become a critical concern.

Exposing APIs directly to the internet can introduce risks such as unauthorized access, data breaches, and denial-of-service attacks. Leveraging SSH tunnels and related techniques, organizations can provide secure and controlled access to APIs while reducing the exposure of sensitive endpoints to public networks.

One common use case for SSH in API security is tunneling API traffic through an encrypted SSH connection. This approach effectively creates a secure channel between the client and the API server, protecting the traffic from eavesdropping and tampering, even over untrusted networks. By forwarding a local port on the client machine to the remote API server via SSH, the API remains hidden from the public internet and accessible only to users or systems with the appropriate SSH credentials. This model is particularly useful in environments where APIs manage sensitive operations such as financial transactions, customer data retrieval, or control of critical infrastructure systems.

For example, a development team working remotely may require access to a private API hosted within a secure corporate network. Instead of opening the API to external IP addresses or deploying a VPN, an SSH tunnel can be established from the developer's machine to a bastion host within the organization. The bastion host then forwards the traffic to the API server located on an internal network. This limits the exposure of the API to only those who can establish an SSH connection, enforcing both network-level and credential-based access control.

Using SSH for secure API access also enhances protection against common attack vectors such as IP spoofing, brute-force attacks, or reconnaissance scans that frequently target public API endpoints. By ensuring that the API is only accessible via the secure tunnel, the attack surface is greatly reduced. Attackers cannot easily probe the API server for vulnerabilities or exploit open ports because it is not reachable from the general internet. In addition to protecting against external threats, this approach adds a layer of defense against insider threats by restricting who can create the tunnel and access the API behind it.

SSH-based access to APIs can be further enhanced through automated workflows. Automation tools and scripts can be configured to programmatically establish SSH tunnels as part of their execution processes. For instance, a CI/CD pipeline running on a build server can open an SSH tunnel to securely interact with an internal API for tasks such as provisioning infrastructure, triggering deployment jobs, or querying system status. By automating tunnel creation and teardown, pipelines can maintain secure and ephemeral connections to APIs, reducing the risk of long-lived tunnels being forgotten and potentially exploited.

In cloud-native environments, where services and APIs are deployed across multiple regions or virtual private clouds (VPCs), SSH is often used in conjunction with bastion hosts or jump servers. A microservice running in one cloud region may need to securely call an API in a different region where direct routing is restricted by firewalls or security groups. Rather than exposing the API externally, the microservice can route its API calls through an SSH tunnel established to a bastion host with access to the private network of the target API. This maintains segmentation between cloud environments while ensuring secure inter-service communication.

SSH tunnels also support secure integration with third-party APIs or services. For instance, in partnerships where two organizations need to exchange data through APIs, SSH tunnels can create secure, encrypted pathways between trusted networks. This allows for direct API calls to be made over the tunnel, bypassing exposure to the public internet. Such an arrangement is particularly valuable in industries like finance or healthcare, where regulatory requirements dictate the use of secure channels for transmitting sensitive data.

Another benefit of using SSH for API access is its compatibility with a wide range of authentication mechanisms. SSH supports public key authentication, certificate-based access, and multi-factor authentication, providing organizations with flexibility to enforce strong identity verification. When combined with API-level authentication schemes such as OAuth2, JWT tokens, or API keys, SSH tunnels provide defense in depth. Even if API credentials are compromised, attackers would still need SSH access to the internal network to exploit them effectively.

While SSH provides significant security benefits for API access, it must be implemented with proper controls to avoid introducing new risks. Tunnels should be configured with limited scope, only forwarding the minimum required ports and destinations. Administrators should avoid enabling unrestricted dynamic port forwarding (SOCKS proxies) unless necessary and should monitor tunnel usage through logging and session auditing. In environments with strict compliance requirements, SSH tunnels should be integrated into centralized access control systems and tied to role-based permissions.

Monitoring is another critical aspect of maintaining secure SSH tunnels for API access. Security teams should implement logging of tunnel creation events, track which users and systems are establishing tunnels, and analyze traffic patterns for signs of misuse or anomaly. Solutions such as SIEM platforms can aggregate logs from SSH servers and provide real-time visibility into tunnel activity. Alerts can be configured to notify administrators if tunnels are being created from unusual IP addresses, at abnormal times, or with unexpected destination targets.

In addition to security, SSH-based API access offers operational flexibility. During development and testing, engineers can securely access APIs hosted in isolated environments without modifying firewall rules or reconfiguring cloud security groups. This accelerates the development lifecycle while maintaining strict access controls. For production environments, SSH tunnels can serve as part of disaster recovery procedures, enabling secure fallback access to critical APIs when other network paths are unavailable due to outages or disruptions.

Finally, SSH tunnels for API access support hybrid cloud and on-premises integrations. As organizations adopt multi-cloud strategies or maintain legacy systems in on-premises data centers, secure communication between disparate environments becomes essential. SSH tunnels facilitate this by bridging private APIs in data centers with cloud workloads in a secure and auditable manner. This is particularly useful for legacy APIs that were never designed to operate securely over the internet but remain critical to business operations.

SSH remains a versatile and powerful tool for securing API access across a wide array of use cases and industries. Its ability to create encrypted tunnels, enforce strong authentication, and operate across heterogeneous environments makes it an essential component of modern API security strategies. When implemented thoughtfully, SSH not only protects sensitive API communications but also enhances agility and resilience in increasingly complex and distributed infrastructures.

SSH in Government and Military Networks

SSH is an indispensable tool in securing communication, remote access, and system management within government and military networks, where data sensitivity and operational security are paramount. In these environments, the integrity, confidentiality, and availability of systems must be guaranteed, given that any compromise could have wide-reaching implications on national security, defense operations, and public safety. Government agencies and military organizations rely on SSH to enable secure administrative control over critical infrastructure, classified networks, and mission-critical applications, ensuring that remote access to sensitive systems is conducted with the highest level of security and accountability.

The use of SSH in government and military networks is rooted in its ability to provide end-to-end encryption for communication channels over untrusted or semi-trusted networks. Whether connecting from one secured military base to another, or accessing remote assets located in geographically isolated regions, SSH enables operators and administrators to manage systems without exposing data to potential interception or tampering. The encrypted tunnel created by SSH ensures that credentials, commands, and system responses remain protected from adversaries, even when traversing potentially compromised or hostile network segments.

Given the heightened threat landscape faced by government and defense organizations, SSH implementations in these environments are subject to stricter standards and controls compared to typical enterprise settings. For example, password-based authentication is almost universally prohibited in favor of key-based or certificate-based authentication, which provides stronger security and eliminates many of the risks associated with password reuse, phishing, or brute-force attacks. SSH keys used in these environments are often generated and managed through hardened systems, with private keys stored on hardware security modules (HSMs) or secure smart cards to prevent theft or unauthorized duplication.

SSH in government and military networks is tightly integrated with broader access control frameworks, such as Public Key Infrastructure (PKI) systems and centralized identity and access management (IAM) platforms. Many agencies and military branches leverage PKI-based SSH certificates to enforce strict identity verification and limit the validity period of credentials, reducing the window of opportunity for misuse. These certificates can include granular attributes, specifying which systems or networks a user can access and under what conditions. By tying SSH authentication to centrally managed directories and role-based access policies, administrators can ensure that only authorized personnel with a verified mission need are permitted to access sensitive systems.

Network segmentation is another critical element when deploying SSH within government and military environments. Sensitive assets are typically isolated within classified or air-gapped networks, segmented from general-purpose IT infrastructure and external internet access. SSH is used to bridge these segmented networks in a controlled manner, often through dedicated bastion hosts or secure gateways that are themselves hardened, monitored, and physically secured. These gateways serve as audit points, logging every SSH session and enforcing additional authentication and authorization steps before granting access to internal systems. In highly classified environments, SSH access may be restricted to pre-approved secure facilities, with strict controls governing who may initiate connections and from where.

SSH also plays a significant role in supporting mission-critical operations, such as remote management of battlefield communication systems, satellite ground stations, and intelligence-gathering platforms. In these scenarios, systems may be deployed in austere or remote environments where direct physical access is not feasible. Through SSH, operators can maintain, troubleshoot, and reconfigure systems from secure command centers while ensuring that data and control channels remain shielded from electronic warfare tactics, signal interception, or cyberattacks.

In addition to operational access, SSH is integral to the automation of system updates, configuration management, and secure file transfers across government networks. Agencies often deploy configuration management tools such as Ansible or SaltStack that rely on SSH to orchestrate secure updates and policy enforcement across distributed systems. Whether applying security patches, deploying new cryptographic policies, or configuring security baselines, SSH provides the backbone for these automation processes. In environments where compliance with frameworks such as NIST SP 800-53, DISA STIGs, or other military standards is mandatory, SSH enables security teams to enforce compliance at scale while maintaining a clear audit trail of administrative actions.

Auditing and accountability are paramount in government and military use of SSH. Every SSH session must be logged in detail, capturing user identities, connection metadata, and executed commands. Logs are typically forwarded to centralized Security Information and Event Management (SIEM) platforms or mission-specific monitoring systems, where they are subject to real-time analysis and long-term retention for forensic purposes. In high-security environments, additional measures such as session recording and keystroke logging may be implemented, ensuring that every action performed over an SSH connection can be reviewed and investigated if necessary.

Advanced threat detection and incident response capabilities are also layered onto SSH workflows within government and military settings. Behavioral analytics, anomaly detection algorithms, and AI-driven security tools continuously monitor SSH session data to detect patterns indicative of insider threats, account compromise, or lateral movement by adversaries. Any suspicious SSH activity—such as unauthorized privilege escalation, abnormal access times, or unexpected remote destinations—can trigger automated alerts and initiate incident response protocols, limiting potential damage before it escalates.

SSH is also critical in supporting joint operations and coalition environments, where interoperability between agencies, branches, or allied forces is essential. Secure communication and remote access protocols must adhere to common standards while respecting each entity's security posture and operational requirements. SSH provides a reliable and flexible means to manage and share access to critical systems across organizational and national boundaries while maintaining strict control over who can access what and when.

Given the sensitivity of the information handled in these environments, SSH usage must also comply with national and international regulations governing classified and controlled unclassified information (CUI). Government policies often dictate that all remote administrative access, including SSH, be conducted using systems that meet specified cryptographic module validation standards, such as FIPS 140-2 or the newer FIPS 140-3. Ensuring that SSH configurations and implementations adhere to these certifications is essential to maintaining compliance and trust within the defense and intelligence communities.

As cyber threats targeting government and military infrastructure continue to evolve, the role of SSH as a secure access mechanism will remain critical. However, it is equally important that agencies continuously assess and update their SSH implementations, integrating emerging security technologies such as quantum-resistant cryptography, zero trust architectures, and machine identity management. SSH will continue to serve as a cornerstone of secure communications in these highly sensitive environments, supporting national security, mission assurance, and operational resilience.

SSH in Financial and Healthcare Systems

SSH plays a vital role in securing financial and healthcare systems, where the confidentiality, integrity, and availability of data are of utmost importance. Both industries deal with highly sensitive information, ranging from patient medical records and clinical data to financial transactions and customer account details. The criticality of these sectors demands robust security measures to protect against cyberattacks, insider threats, and compliance violations. SSH provides a secure method for remote administration, secure file transfers, and encrypted communications between servers, databases, and various interconnected systems within these industries.

In financial institutions, SSH is widely used to manage critical infrastructure such as banking servers, payment gateways, transaction processors, and financial databases. These components must be maintained with the highest levels of security due to the constant threat posed by cybercriminals seeking to gain unauthorized access to financial assets or sensitive data. SSH provides secure encrypted channels for system administrators, database administrators, and DevOps teams to manage systems and deploy updates without exposing sensitive credentials or data to interception over public or internal networks.

SSH also serves as a key mechanism for transferring sensitive financial data between systems. Financial institutions routinely transfer transaction records, customer data, reports, and regulatory filings across internal networks or to third-party partners. Using SCP or SFTP, which both leverage SSH for encryption and authentication, ensures that data in transit remains protected against eavesdropping, tampering, or unauthorized access. This is especially critical when exchanging data with external stakeholders, such as regulatory bodies or partner financial institutions, where secure channels must be maintained to comply with regulations such as PCI DSS, SOX, and GLBA.

In the healthcare industry, SSH is indispensable for securing systems that store and process protected health information (PHI). Electronic Health Record (EHR) systems, laboratory information systems, medical imaging servers, and hospital administration systems all require secure remote administration capabilities. Healthcare organizations rely on SSH to ensure that IT staff and third-party vendors can securely access these systems to perform necessary maintenance, troubleshooting, and updates, especially in distributed healthcare networks that include remote clinics, laboratories, and telemedicine platforms.

Compliance with industry regulations is a driving force behind SSH usage in healthcare environments. Regulations such as the Health Insurance Portability and Accountability Act (HIPAA) mandate strict safeguards for PHI, including secure transmission mechanisms and access controls. SSH helps healthcare organizations meet these requirements by providing secure, auditable remote access and file transfer capabilities. Additionally, SSH can be integrated with centralized identity and access management systems to enforce role-based access controls, ensuring that only authorized healthcare staff or IT personnel can access sensitive systems.

Both financial and healthcare sectors benefit from the ability of SSH to support strong authentication mechanisms. In environments where password policies alone are insufficient, SSH key-based authentication or SSH certificates provide a higher level of security by requiring cryptographic credentials. In many cases, private keys are stored on hardware security modules (HSMs), smart cards, or secure elements within endpoint devices, further protecting against key theft or compromise. Multi-factor authentication (MFA) is often layered on top of SSH access workflows, adding an additional verification step before access is granted to critical systems.

In financial systems, SSH plays a key role in securing automated processes, such as overnight batch jobs, settlement processing, and transaction reconciliation tasks. These processes often involve scripts and applications that connect to remote servers to execute time-sensitive operations. SSH enables these automated systems to operate securely without human intervention, using secure keys or certificates managed through centralized credential management systems. The secure channels provided by SSH also ensure the integrity of these transactions, which may involve the movement of large sums of money or sensitive financial records.

Similarly, healthcare environments depend on automated workflows secured by SSH for tasks such as nightly EHR database backups, data synchronization between healthcare facilities, and secure uploads of diagnostic imaging to cloud storage platforms. Automation enhances operational efficiency and reduces the manual burden on healthcare IT staff, while SSH ensures that these automated processes maintain compliance with security and privacy standards.

Monitoring and auditing SSH usage is critical in both financial and healthcare settings. Security teams must have full visibility into SSH activity, including which users accessed which systems, when, and what actions were performed. In financial institutions, failure to properly monitor SSH sessions can lead to regulatory penalties if unauthorized access to financial systems goes undetected. In healthcare, unauthorized access to PHI through unmonitored SSH sessions could result in HIPAA violations, patient privacy breaches, and significant legal and reputational damage.

To address these risks, organizations implement centralized logging systems to capture SSH session data, with logs forwarded to Security Information and Event Management (SIEM) platforms for analysis and alerting. Some institutions deploy session recording tools that capture terminal outputs of SSH sessions, allowing for detailed forensic investigations if suspicious activity is detected. SSH gateways, or bastion hosts, are often used as chokepoints for SSH traffic, providing a centralized access point where logging, authentication enforcement, and session monitoring can be applied uniformly.

SSH also plays a role in disaster recovery and incident response processes within financial and healthcare systems. In the event of a security breach, infrastructure failure, or data center outage, SSH enables IT teams to securely connect to backup systems, isolated recovery environments, or cloud-based disaster recovery sites to restore services and ensure business continuity. The secure nature of SSH ensures that sensitive data and administrative actions remain protected during the recovery process, even when operations are being conducted over emergency communication channels or temporary network configurations.

Despite the security benefits provided by SSH, both financial and healthcare organizations must be vigilant against the misuse of SSH tunnels, which can be exploited to bypass network segmentation controls or create covert communication channels. Security policies must clearly define acceptable use cases for SSH tunneling and forwarding, and technical controls should be implemented to restrict or audit tunnel usage. This helps prevent insider threats or external attackers from leveraging SSH tunnels to exfiltrate sensitive data or access systems outside of approved workflows.

The critical nature of financial transactions and patient data means that SSH configurations in these industries must be hardened to the highest standards. SSH servers should enforce strict cipher suites, disable legacy protocols such as SSHv1, and limit access to trusted IP ranges. Automated key rotation and regular access reviews help ensure that only necessary and authorized keys remain active, reducing the risk of unauthorized access through stale or forgotten credentials.

SSH is a foundational element of secure operations within financial and healthcare systems, supporting secure remote access, data transfer, automation, and incident response. When implemented alongside comprehensive access controls, monitoring, and compliance frameworks, SSH helps protect sensitive assets while enabling operational efficiency in environments where the stakes are high and the tolerance for security breaches is virtually zero.

The Human Factor: SSH and Social Engineering

SSH is a cornerstone of secure remote access and system administration, designed to protect against unauthorized access and ensure encrypted communication over insecure networks. Its cryptographic strength makes it difficult for attackers to break directly through brute-force or cryptographic attacks, especially when properly configured. However, no matter how secure a protocol is, the human element often becomes the weakest link. Social engineering attacks, which exploit human behavior rather than technical vulnerabilities, are increasingly used by attackers to compromise SSH access, bypass security controls, and gain footholds within critical infrastructure.

Social engineering targets individuals, manipulating them into divulging sensitive information, clicking malicious links, or performing actions that undermine security protocols. SSH, while robust at the protocol level, is susceptible to such human-centered attacks when users or administrators are coerced or deceived into compromising their private keys, passwords, or security practices. One of the most common scenarios occurs when attackers use phishing emails to impersonate trusted entities, such as IT administrators, system alerts, or even executives. These emails often urge recipients to urgently share SSH keys or passwords, claiming that immediate access is needed for a critical patch, troubleshooting, or compliance verification.

A particularly effective technique used by attackers is spear phishing, where emails are highly personalized based on reconnaissance of the target's role, responsibilities, or relationships within the organization. For example, a system administrator might receive an email appearing to come from a colleague in another department, requesting urgent assistance with server access. In moments of pressure or distraction, even experienced administrators may overlook red flags and unknowingly share SSH private keys or grant temporary access to malicious actors.

Attackers may also employ pretexting, a tactic in which they create a fabricated scenario to persuade their target to lower their guard. An attacker could call a help desk impersonating a senior executive, claiming to be locked out of critical systems and demanding immediate SSH access. In high-stakes environments where employees may feel pressured to comply with authority figures or prioritize business continuity, such scenarios can successfully bypass well-established access control policies.

Another area where social engineering intersects with SSH is in the manipulation of supply chains and third-party vendors. Contractors and external service providers often require SSH access to an organization's systems for legitimate maintenance or development tasks. Attackers may impersonate these trusted vendors or compromise their accounts to gain SSH credentials that provide direct access to the target's infrastructure. Once inside, attackers can leverage the access to move laterally within the network, escalate privileges, and exfiltrate sensitive data.

The compromise of SSH keys is one of the most dangerous outcomes of successful social engineering. Unlike passwords, SSH private keys are often unprotected by passphrases or stored insecurely on endpoint devices. An attacker who convinces a user to share a private key, or who gains remote access to a device through malware or phishing, can reuse the key across multiple servers if proper key management policies are not in place. This is particularly problematic in environments where SSH key sprawl is prevalent and where keys are reused across systems without proper segmentation or expiration controls.

Social engineering campaigns may also aim to trick users into installing malicious tools or modifying SSH configurations. For instance, an attacker might convince a target to install a remote troubleshooting tool disguised as legitimate software, which silently replaces the system's sshd binary or installs a malicious SSH backdoor. In such cases, even if SSH keys and user credentials remain secure, the compromised SSH service could log and exfiltrate authentication attempts, keystrokes, or session data without detection.

Defending against the human factor requires a combination of technical controls and continuous user education. Organizations must train their staff to recognize common social engineering tactics, such as phishing, pretexting, baiting, and tailgating, emphasizing the importance of skepticism when handling unexpected access requests. Employees should be trained to verify the legitimacy of SSH-related requests through secondary communication channels, such as calling a known contact directly instead of responding to an email request.

In addition to awareness training, organizations should enforce strict SSH key management practices. Every SSH key should be tied to an individual identity, with unique keys for each user and system. Keys should be rotated regularly, protected with strong passphrases, and stored securely. Furthermore, access to critical systems via SSH should be governed by the principle of least privilege, limiting what each user or process can access. Multi-factor authentication (MFA) can also mitigate the risk of stolen credentials or compromised keys, as attackers would still require the additional authentication factor to gain access.

Technical controls such as centralized access logging, SIEM integration, and session monitoring play an essential role in detecting anomalies resulting from successful social engineering attempts. For example, if an attacker leverages a stolen SSH key to access a production system outside of business hours from an unfamiliar IP address, security teams should be alerted automatically. Similarly, commands executed during SSH sessions can be monitored to identify suspicious behavior, such as attempts to modify user accounts, alter SSH configurations, or disable security monitoring tools.

The human factor also extends to developers and DevOps teams who may inadvertently introduce risks by embedding SSH keys into scripts, configuration files, or code repositories. Attackers frequently scan public and private repositories for exposed keys, which can then be used to target SSH services. Promoting secure coding practices and conducting regular security audits of repositories is crucial to reducing this risk.

Ultimately, while SSH is a powerful and secure protocol, its effectiveness depends heavily on how it is used by the people who rely on it daily. Attackers will continue to exploit human tendencies—such as trust, fear, urgency, and unfamiliarity with evolving threats—to circumvent technical defenses. By fostering a security-aware culture and implementing layered security controls, organizations can significantly reduce the likelihood that social engineering attacks will lead to the compromise of SSH credentials or the systems they protect. The convergence of human vigilance and robust technical defenses is essential to maintaining the integrity of SSH-reliant infrastructure in an era where attackers increasingly target people rather than machines.

The Future of SSH in a Connected World

In an increasingly connected world where digital transformation is reshaping industries, SSH remains one of the most trusted and essential tools for securing remote access and communication. As networks expand, cloud computing becomes ubiquitous, and organizations integrate more automation into their operations, SSH will continue to play a foundational role. However, the future of SSH is not static; it is poised to evolve in response to emerging security challenges, technological advancements, and shifting operational paradigms.

The global move towards hybrid and multi-cloud environments has already introduced complexities that demand more adaptable and scalable remote access solutions. SSH's flexibility has allowed it to thrive in this changing landscape, enabling secure connections across on-premises data centers, cloud infrastructure, and containerized applications. As businesses increasingly rely on cloud service providers and distributed infrastructure, the ability of SSH to bridge these diverse environments securely has become more critical than ever. In the coming years, we can expect to see SSH integrated even more tightly with cloud-native tools, identity and access management systems, and Infrastructure as Code frameworks to automate access while maintaining security.

Automation will continue to drive much of SSH's future development. With the widespread adoption of DevOps and continuous integration/continuous deployment (CI/CD) pipelines, SSH is already a key enabler of secure automation. However, to meet the growing demand for speed and scale, organizations will move toward further automating SSH key management, certificate issuance, and session initiation. This will reduce human error, minimize key sprawl, and ensure that secure practices are consistently applied across increasingly large and complex infrastructures. The shift toward short-lived, ephemeral SSH certificates rather than long-term static keys will likely become more prevalent, as it aligns with modern security principles such as zero trust and least privilege.

The zero trust security model will continue to influence SSH's evolution. Traditionally, SSH has been deployed in environments where access was restricted based on network perimeter controls. However, as zero trust gains traction, organizations are rethinking how they authorize and authenticate users and systems. In this model, SSH will increasingly serve as part of identity-aware access controls, where user context, device health, and real-time risk assessments dictate who is allowed to establish an SSH session. SSH gateways and bastion hosts will evolve to incorporate zero trust principles, enforcing dynamic policies and integrating more deeply with authentication providers, threat intelligence feeds, and behavioral analytics engines.

Security concerns, particularly those associated with SSH key management, will drive further innovation. Poorly managed SSH keys remain a common vulnerability in many organizations, leading to unauthorized access, insider threats, and audit failures. The future of SSH will likely see broader adoption of centralized SSH key management platforms that automate the discovery, rotation, and revocation of keys across environments. In addition, cloud providers and third-party vendors will continue to expand offerings that abstract away traditional SSH key management, providing secure, ephemeral access through API-driven solutions and IAM integration.

Emerging technologies, such as quantum computing, will also impact the future of SSH. The development of quantum computers capable of breaking current public key cryptographic algorithms, including RSA and ECDSA, has prompted research into post-quantum cryptography (PQC). SSH will need to evolve by adopting quantum-resistant key exchange and authentication algorithms to ensure that encrypted sessions remain secure in a post-quantum world. Experimental support for lattice-based algorithms, such as NTRU and Kyber, has already been introduced into some SSH implementations, and the trend will continue as standards for post-quantum cryptography are finalized and adopted globally.

SSH will also adapt to better serve the growing world of edge computing and the Internet of Things (IoT). In an era where billions of devices are connected to networks, securing remote access to edge nodes and IoT devices is essential. SSH's lightweight nature and wide platform support make it well-suited for managing edge devices, but enhancements in scalability and automation will be required. SSH will increasingly be used to secure communications between edge nodes and centralized management systems, supporting operations such as remote diagnostics, software updates, and real-time monitoring in industries ranging from smart cities to industrial automation.

Another area where SSH will evolve is in addressing the increasing demand for compliance and auditability. Organizations in regulated industries such as finance, healthcare, and critical infrastructure must comply with stringent data protection and access control requirements. Future SSH deployments will incorporate more advanced session monitoring, real-time alerting, and forensic logging capabilities to meet these regulatory demands. Integration with SIEM platforms and security orchestration tools will become standard, providing end-to-end visibility into SSH activity across distributed environments.

The continued rise of containers and microservices will also shape SSH's trajectory. While container orchestration platforms such as Kubernetes rely primarily on API-driven management, SSH still plays a role in securing access to the underlying infrastructure. Future SSH enhancements will focus on providing secure, automated access to ephemeral environments while reducing the need for long-lived SSH keys. Developers and operators will rely more on temporary credentials and automated workflows that limit manual SSH usage while preserving its availability for debugging, emergency maintenance, or troubleshooting.

The role of SSH in disaster recovery and incident response will remain critical. In scenarios where automated systems fail or security incidents require manual intervention, SSH provides a reliable and secure fallback mechanism for administrators to access and remediate systems. Future developments will likely include improved support for securely accessing isolated or air-gapped environments, where SSH may be used in conjunction with secure transfer protocols and physical security measures.

SSH's role as a trusted protocol in secure remote administration, file transfer, and automation is firmly entrenched, but its future is dynamic and adaptable. As security threats evolve and IT environments become more complex, SSH will continue to serve as a cornerstone of secure connectivity. However, its success will depend on how well organizations adapt to new technologies, integrate automation, and align SSH usage with modern security frameworks and operational requirements. The future of SSH lies not only in its protocol-level enhancements but also in its seamless integration into the broader fabric of cybersecurity and IT infrastructure management.

www.ingramcontent.com/pod-product-compliance
Lightning Source LLC
La Vergne TN
LVHW051235050326
832903LV00028B/2416